"... Positive, practical and enjoyable. A must read for any single father."

STEPHEN FINSTEIN, LMSW-ACP, LMFT, RSOTP, MARRIAGE AND FAMILY THERAPIST, MENTAL HEALTH ADVISOR

"Male single parenting in a humorous, positive and practical way."

ANDREW SCHULTZ, L.P.C., SINGLE FATHER

"... I commend Mr. Hoerner for presenting a realistic approach to cooperative parenting."

DEBRA LEHRMANN, JUDGE, 360TH DISTRICT COURT, TARRANT COUNTY, TEXAS

"... Very Fresh, Informative, and Insightful! As a single mother, it is necessary to know that fathers face the same challenges that women do. It is of the utmost importance that both men and women realize the similarities that will allow them to empathize with one another, in order to create a positive presence in the lives of their children, as well as their own."

KARYN GRACE, A SINGLE MOM FROM CHICAGO

The Ultimate Survival Guide
FOR THE
SINGLE FATHER

Thomas Hoerner

Harbinger Press

Published simultaneously in Canada.

Harbinger Press
2711 Buford Rd., PMB 383
Richmond, VA 23235
804-560-1195
www.harbpress.com

Illustrations by Patrick David,
Lords of Design, New York, New York

Cover and Interior Design and Typesetting by
Desktop Miracles, Inc., Stowe, Vermont

Publisher's Cataloging-in-Publication
(Provided by Quality Books, Inc.)

Hoerner, Thomas
    The ultimate survival guide for the single father / Thomas
Hoerner. — 1st ed.
    p.   cm.
    Includes bibliographical references.
    LCCN 2001076060
    ISBN 0–9674736–4–0

    1. Single fathers—Life skills guides   2. Parenting.   I. Title

HQ759.915.H64   2002   306.85'6
                                                      QBI01-201325

Important Note to the Reader

Formerly published under the titled *Bachelor Parents and their Functional Families.*

Contents

Topic Index

Acknowledgments

To my ex-wife and the mother of my children, Sonia. Thank you for giving me the finest treasures of my life. Your unselfish decision has allowed me to be the father I am today.

To my mother and father, for teaching me to love, giving me enduring values, and helping me succeed in life. I love you both. Mom, I miss you.

To my sons, Thomas (T.J.), Justin, and Stephen. You are my pals, my reason for being, and my greatest asset in life. I am proud of each of you. Remember any thing is possible when you believe. Be happy. I love you.

To Todd Wendt and the late Jim Marquart. Two friends and past supervisors who allowed me to realign my career, adjust my priorities, and be a dad. Without your understanding and compassion, I would have missed my purpose in life.

To Brenda Martin, my dear friend, who believed in me when others thought I was nuts. Your friendship through the years has been priceless. Thanks for being there.

To Thomas Bedell, my editor and instructor. This book would not have been possible without your help and guidance. Cheers!

To Jeanne Kastler, my girlfriend. Thank you for your continued encouragement, your genuine interest, and your unselfish support. This book and my life would be incomplete without you.

This time we got it right!

Introduction

Prior to gaining primary custody of my three sons in January 1992, I led the single life of a divorced man and enjoyed a rewarding career. I traveled about 70 percent of the time, lived alone in a nice apartment, and accepted my role as a visiting parent. Regrettably, there were times I lived as far as 1,200 miles away from my children and I wound up spending a fortune trying to visit them from Chicago to San Antonio every four to eight weeks.

After a year of commuting, I transferred to Dallas to be closer to my children. Three months later my ex-wife asked, "How would you feel about the boys coming to live with you?" I immediately, without thinking, said, "Yes!"

Almost as instantly, my mind was flooded with a bombardment of obstacles I would face if my children lived with me. What about my job? How would I travel? Who would care for the boys when I worked? What about my social life? Would I be able to provide for my children? What if the boys didn't like living with me?

My fears and anxieties grew. I tried to stay optimistic by focusing on the positive aspects of having custody, like not having to follow my ex–wife's commands regarding my children, and I certainly enjoyed the thought of not paying child support anymore.

Over the next several months I negotiated a new arrangement with my ex–wife. Each discussion was the same. She was hesitant to sign the children over to me because of what I believe was predictable guilt and shame, and I would not assume custody on a temporary basis. It would be just my luck to rearrange my career path, buy a home, and have her say, "I've changed my mind."

Although I was eager to assume the role as the primary care provider, I have to admit that every time I said, "Sign the papers and the children can move in with me," more obstacles arose in my mind. How would I find a sitter? Did I make enough money to support us? Where would we live? What is it like to raise children alone?

Talk about stress and anxieties. The only relief I had was that part of me believed my ex–wife would never actually give me custody. Then, to my surprise one October day, she said, "I'll sign the papers and allow the boys to live with you." (At that point, 300 miles away from her.) I was about to accept a major task that was going to change my life dramatically.

Would it have eased my mind then knowing that there were more than a million other single males like me with custody of their children? It wouldn't have hurt.

According to Census Bureau statistics regarding *Marital Status and Living Arrangements* (March 2000), men with custody of their children now total close to three million households. And this number will continue to grow as new gender-free family laws are written and custody is awarded to the parent best able to care for the children.

In addition, there are a growing number of women voluntarily giving up custody to pursue career goals. Quite a reversal on traditional values.

Custodial men are not the only men trying to create a home environment for their children. Fathers take a bad rap because of the number of men who walk away from their children, but the actual number of involved fathers shows just the opposite. Census Bureau statistics also show there are over eight million fathers who, in addition to paying child support, participate in their children's lives.

From the day my ex-wife agreed to our new custody arrangement, I had two months to prepare. When the day we were to switch custody roles came, I drove from Dallas to San Antonio to pick up my three sons. Typically, I used this time in the car to plan my visit, reflect on my current agenda, and listen to my favorite music. It was usually a relaxing ride. This trip was different.

More doubts entered my mind. How do I discipline a child? How do I buy children's clothes? How do I shop for groceries? What will I cook for dinner? *What the hell was I doing?* My heart beat faster, my feet tapped nervously, and my sweaty palms clutched the steering wheel until they hurt. This was truly the longest ride of my life!

Gaining custody is difficult for men, so I was extremely fortunate when it came about uncontested, and long after my divorce. I was over the wounds of a failed relationship and the scars from a long court battle had healed. I was well-adjusted to my life and able to enter my custodial role in an eager and positive frame of mind. I also had a desire to be with my children. Other men approach the situation in different ways, and, unfortunately, bitterness can make the adjustment period more difficult.

At the time I took custody, my three sons were three, seven, and ten. Today Stephen, my youngest, is thirteen, Justin is seventeen, Thomas (T.J.) is twenty, and they have made me earn a B.S. degree from the Hoerner Home Institute of Domestic Engineering and Family Development Center. I specialize in juggling a career, family, and social calendar. I have learned to raise trouble-free children in a troubled world. I have mastered the art of attending a football game and a choir recital simultaneously. I have fought in courts over custody and domicile, and I have been forced to pass up promotions due to my commitments to my children. I have loved and hated my ex-wife. I have been Santa, the Easter Bunny, and the Tooth Fairy. I have sat with sick children and heard a baby cry for his mother. I have experienced everything from toilet-training to puberty, and at one time all this scared the hell out of me!

Can all this stress, anxiety, sacrifice, and extra work possibly be rewarding? Yes. The benefits far outweigh the slight inconveniences. The first time a date is canceled because of a sick child is soon forgotten when he draws a picture that says, "Dad, I love you." It's this love between a father and his children that overcomes all obstacles and brings immeasurable satisfaction.

This book is for single fathers and any male parents who face the challenges of raising children while balancing a career, home, and social life. It's the official owner's manual for raising children and living a healthy life. The topics discussed are entirely from a single father's perspective and focus on practical solutions to everyday problems. There is also occasional humor.

Until now, a single father would have to buy several books for all the topics found in *Single Father*. That's not very feasible for anyone on a limited budget and time schedule. Also, much of what has been previously written on these subjects is for women, and portrays fathers as visiting parents or absent altogether. This is for men who are on the scene.

The book is put together in such a way that if you need help in a certain area fast, just turn to the particular chapter for direct advice that should immediately lessen your panic. Can't cook, for example? Turn to Chapter 9. Want to date on a limited budget? See Chapter 16.

So, relax and enjoy. There are no tests to measure skills, and no one expects perfection. Measure success entirely by your happiness and that of your children. Put things into perspective: Understanding an internal combustion engine is hard. By comparison, being a single parent is, well, not as hard.

Pre-Divorce

R on, a father of two, recalls his custody battle. "I spent $20,000 in attorneys' fees and in return I was screwed by our court system.

"My wife left me to raise our children while she abused drugs and ran around like a whore. When I filed for divorce and custody, she quickly countered and made child abuse accusations. I thought, how could a judge award custody to a woman like this? Everyone agreed with me, even the attorney I found on page 147 of the yellow pages.

"My wife's attorney, a real-man hater, presented a case of lies, false testimonies, and unsubstantiated abuse. Before I knew what happened, Child Protective Services stepped in. My children were removed from my home, placed in their mother's care, and I was exiled from their life, except for paying child support. My God, my children even had their own attorney."

Emotionally destroyed, Ron continued his battle and after nine months of turmoil was awarded one supervised visit a week. "Some visitation. My children and I were placed in a 12' by 12' room and supervised by an official of the court. How demeaning. I felt like a prisoner, afraid to touch my own children."

Ron's successful business was ruined by anonymous phone calls to his customers asking, "Are you aware you are dealing with a child molester?" These accusations of child abuse slandered Ron's professional image and led to the end of his career.

"I don't mind losing my business as much as I do my children," he says. "But my biggest fear is that my children might start believing all the lies my ex-wife has made up and I will lose them forever."

Jim, a single father with joint custody of two girls, has his own war story. "When my divorce was over I thought, I am finally done with her! Little did I know the next 15 years would be a roller coaster ride through the legal system. My ex is so possessed with making my life miserable, she takes me back to court every other year to raise my child support."

Ron's and Jim's living nightmares are shared by many. And though this book focuses on post-divorce scenarios, pre-divorce and court room advice seems appropriate here, just in case.

Join a Father's Rights Group

With the assistance of a father's group, a father can save thousands of dollars in attorney's fees and avoid poor legal representation. Most organizations are nonprofit and offer education in law, parenting classes, referrals of attorneys, mediators, typists, private investigators, mental health advisors, process services, and support.

The National Fathers Resource Center (NFRC), a division of Fathers for Equal Rights (FER), is one such organization dedicated to helping fathers and children obtain favorable resolutions of pre- and post-divorce problems. You may visit FER's website www.fathers4kids.org, for assistance in finding the chapter or organization nearest you. In Canada, there is Fathers Are Capable Too, www.fact.on.ca.

Learn Your Rights

Don't think uncle Lou is an expert in law because he went through a divorce three years ago. A father in a divorce or custody battle must know his rights, or he will be unable to recognize if his attorney is performing properly.

Joining a father's rights group is, again, one way to be informed. However, there are also a number of books written on the topic, and many are available through FER's web page. Of particular value is *Fathers' Rights* (Perseus Books, 1998) by attorney Jeffery M. Leving with Kenneth A. Dachman, tracing real-life examples through every aspect of the custody process from the courts to therapists' couches. Pick one up and read it. Knowledge is power.

Find A Good Attorney

The best advice on selecting an attorney comes from therapist Stephen D. Finstein, LMSW-ACP, LMFT, Mental Health Advisor and Director, National Fathers' Resource Center (NFRC): "Don't just open a phone book and pick one, and don't hire an attorney just because he/she did a will for your uncle or helped a family member in criminal case. Family law is a special area. Representing a father is usually an uphill battle and takes special skills (*e.g.*, handling false child abuse, sex abuse, and domestic violence accusations). In smaller communities, lawyers may do a general practice (civil, criminal, etc.) and you may have no choice. But, in a large city, if you hire a criminal attorney to handle your custody case, expect to be disappointed."

⚖️ Begin your search with a visit to the Election Office (or City Record Office) in your town and pull the election files on the judge(s) who are, or could be, handling your case. Then start the selection process with attorneys who have made campaign contributions. Finding an attorney who is close to the judge is very important.

Experience shows it's better to have an attorney who is *friendly* with the judge.

⚖️ Use personal referrals from friends, other attorneys, judges, and fathers' groups. There is a tremendous list of fathers' organizations and attorney referrals at the Fathers for Equal Rights website, www.fathers4kids.org.

⚖️ Talk to the Court Clerk who works for the judge hearing your case. Ask the clerk for two or three recommendations for a good, affordable attorney who is respected by the judge.

⚖️ Check with attorneys in nearby towns and communities. They can often recommend colleagues in your community who believe in fathers. Caution: Do not hire an attorney from another town unless there are no other alternatives. Judges, especially in small towns, don't like cocky lawyers from outside their communities coming in and beating up on their local lawyers. The "home town advantage" can be very important.

⚖️ Ask local private investigators and process servers for their recommendations.

⚖️ Visit your public or court-house library and research *The Martindale-Hubbell Law Directory*. Interview several attorneys, including those you can't afford. Find the attorneys who are the top guns in your community. Many will give a free or low cost consultation. This is an opportunity to pick their brains. Remember, these are experts, so don't refuse a free consultation. Let them think that you can come up with the money from a rich relative if you like their game plan. Take notes and write down ideas they share with you. Ask them which other attorneys they might recommend to handle your case, especially with a particular judge, or given your wife's attorney. This should give you some strategy ideas and some leads on other attorneys.

⚖ No matter how an attorney is selected, be sure to check his or her credentials with the state licensing board.

⚖ Manage your attorney. Give them their instructions in writing. And don't hesitate to fire them if they fail to follow your directions.

Children and the Beginning of Separation

Tom came home to an empty house. From the moment he opened the door he knew something was wrong. The note on the table read, "Dear Tom, I'm sorry I have to leave. I guess I wasn't cut out to be a parent and a wife. Take care of the children and yourself." Tom was devastated. He was now a single parent against his will.

That same day, David and his wife agreed that their relationship was not working and that he should move out. David was anxious to start dating but promised he would visit the children when he "got it together."

Across town, Jerry discovered his girlfriend of only six months was pregnant and wanted to get married. Jerry and marriage went together like pickles and ice cream. His first thought was, "Hey, it's not mine. I'm outta here."

It would be impossible to address all the situations each of us have experienced ending our relationships. However, regardless of the circumstances, the start of a new living arrangement is difficult for all involved, especially children.

So, before indulging in the problems we face as fathers, let's consider our children. After all, it's their well-being that should be first and foremost. But, frankly, putting children at the top of one's priorities list may be hard for some men to do, especially if one's life is filled with anger, hate, fear, guilt, confusion, grief, or loneliness from a broken relationship. And while these sensations are understandable, they're not excuses to lose control. It's important to create a safe, stable environment for the children as soon as possible, or adjustment for them will be even more difficult.

Stephen D. Finstein says, "Most children have some difficulties at the start of a new custody arrangement and a father should watch for any sudden changes in his child's behavior. Dad should also be aware that it's common for siblings of different ages or sex to have different reactions." Here are some warning signs:

- Substantial anxiety and an inability to relax
- Frequent ailments
- Ceaseless denial of their mother's absence

- Lethargic behavior
- Uncontrollable anger or fits
- Unprovoked fighting
- Persistent seclusion
- Lingering guilt and self-blame
- Losing interest in activities
- Regressive behavior
- Eating problems
- Chronic depression
- Sleeping problems and/or nightmares
- Poor self-esteem
- Suicidal thoughts
- Drug and alcohol use

Reactions Children May Exhibit By Age

Infant To Two Years Old

At this age, children are normally unaware and unaffected as long as their nurturers and nurturing are constant.

Two To Four Years

During this time period, children may regress in development and behavior. Some examples of outgrown behavior may include their returning to diapers, wetting their pants, or sucking their thumb. Eating problems, such as loss of appetite, may develop. They may also fantasize about reconciliation between the parents.

Three To Six Years

Children at this age may have feelings of fear, helplessness, and instability. This may lead to regressive behavior, sleeping problems, changed eating habits, and guilt. It is hard for some children at this age to accept divorce (or death) because of their idealistic views on two-parent homes, and they may spend a lot of time wondering why Mom left.

Six To Eight Years

At this critical age, many children have feelings of helplessness, guilt, grief, and fear that Dad will also leave. This may lead to regressive behavior or a noticeable change in eating and sleeping patterns. Some children may hang onto an unrealistic hope for reconciliation between their parents or suffer from denial that their mother is gone. Others, especially in the presence of outside influences, may side with one parent.

Eight To Twelve Years

Anger may drive children's behavior at this age. This anger may be directed toward one or both parents, especially if children blame themselves for the divorce. Anger may also surface toward siblings. And anger isn't the only emotion they feel. Many children feel helplessness, anxiety, and guilt. These emotions can create chronic eating and sleeping disorders, or social and emotional problems.

Twelve To Eighteen Years

The effects of living with dad at this age depend highly on the maturity of the child. Some children are almost unaffected by divorce. Yet others develop rebellious behaviors, become unsympathetic toward one or both parents, suffer poor self-esteem, and develop negative attitudes concerning relationships.

This adjustment period may vary. Expect the first year to be the hardest. If problems seem out of control, seek help. Professional counseling is available, often without cost, through a family service agency, mental health agency, doctor, minister, priest, or rabbi. The good news is that few children suffer emotional trauma and regressive behavior after joining their father. Many improve their lives greatly.

A father can help his children adjust by sharing at least 10 to 15 minutes a day talking about how they feel. Listen, offer understanding, and focus on the positive. Be affectionate (nurture them), and tell them, "I love you, and I will always be here for you." Stay honest and answer their questions clearly and on their level. Telling untruths only creates problems that will appear later. Reassure children that the divorce or separation was not their fault and *never* give false hope of reconciliation. If the children's mother is involved, assure them that their mother loves them and that she will remain a part of their lives, too. Expect children to miss their mother and *never* belittle her in their eyes. Understand that their mother is a part of them. When a father says, "Your mother is no good," he is also saying a part of the child is no good. Let's face it, over half of today's marriages fail, which means there are a large number of children growing up with one parent. All children from a broken home, however, are not unhappy, nor do they all grow up to be delinquents. I believe children are stronger than we give them credit for, and at times are restricted (consciously or unconsciously) by the limits and goals set for them. Because children are easily influenced and believe what they are told, telling a child good things is advantageous to keeping a child's outlook positive.

One final thought on divorce: *it sucks!* The associated turmoil often provokes some fathers to act out of anger and without thought. Many of these actions, or should I say reactions, cause some fathers to act selfishly and cruelly.

I must admit there were times when I was consumed by my emotions, out of control, and unaware of the feelings of others. For instance, my early emotional outbursts and derogatory remarks concerning my children's mother were by no means productive and hardly the behavior I would want them to model. My tantrums did nothing but result in additional worries, frustrations, and regrets which I still feel today.

Negative reactions such as these violate our children's rights and cause emotional scars.

To protect children's rights, especially at the time of divorce, the Dane County Family Court Counseling Services in Madison, Wisconsin developed the following Children's Bill of Rights, and we would do well to abide by each and every one:

Children's Bill of Rights

As they proceed with the process of dissolving their relationship, both parents recognize and acknowledge the following minimum rights of their children:

1. Right to a continuing relationship with both parents.

2. Right to be treated as an important human being with unique feelings, ideas, and desires.

3. Right to continuing care and guidance from both parents.

4. Right to know and appreciate what is good in each parent without one parent degrading the other.

5. Right to express love, affection, and respect for each parent without having to stifle that love because of fear and disapproval by the other parent.

6. Right to know that the parents' decision to live separately was not the responsibility of the child.

7. Right not to be a source of argument between the parents.

8. Right to honest answers to questions about the changing family relationships.

9. Right to be able to experience regular and constant contact with both parents and to know the reason for cancellation of visits or change of plans.

10. Right to have a relaxed, secure relationship with both parents without being placed in a position to manipulate one parent against the other.

The Single Father

The day I arrived home with my children was a Sunday, halfway through a two-week school break. My kids were out of school, and I had to work in less then 12 hours! What about my job? My career was in full bloom and I was on my way up. What was I to do? I had business trips starting in a week. Who was going to watch my children? Luckily, I had a friend who would help for a few days while I enrolled them in school and found permanent day-care for my three-year-old. But how was I going to arrange my new life in that short of a time?

We unpacked and tried to settle in by watching TV and making several trips to an empty refrigerator. At times, we sat in awkward silence. We tried to ignore it, but I could tell everyone was nervous about our new situation. That night I lay in bed and stared at the ceiling I was beginning to know so well. I thought about my job, my past relationship with my ex-wife, and the responsibilities that remained ahead. As I drifted into a restless sleep, I thought, *"What the hell am I going to do now?"* Fortunately I found this prayer. I keep it nearby and read it when fears are about to over take me.

A Single Parent's Prayer

Lord Grant Me

Time enough to do all the chores,
join in the games, help with the lessons,
say the night prayers, and much more.

Strength enough to be bread baker
and bread winner,
knee patcher and peace maker,
ball player and bill juggler.

Hands soft enough to hug and to hold,
to tickle and touch,
yet strong enough to pick up
and put away, and then to iron and fold.

Heart enough to share and to care,
to listen and to understand,
and to make this home the best
a single parent can.

UNKNOWN

Ask men what it means to be a father and most reply, "It means spending time with your child." Well, that helps a lot, but showing up is only part of it. Imagine being in a relationship with a woman and just showing up for sex, but otherwise not contributing anything. Not a great return on that. The same holds true with being a father. The best rewards are from the efforts put forth.

In addition to play time, the time spent with a child should be used teaching right from wrong, instilling basic values of self-respect and pride, and living by the Golden Rule, "Do unto others as you would have them do unto you."

In turn, the rewards are immeasurable. There's no replacement for the words, "Dad, I love you!" or the memory of "Look Dad, I caught it!" In addition, the accomplishment of raising good children is considered a noble act (especially in a woman's eyes) and adds an overwhelming boost to a father's self-esteem.

Need help being a dad? The National Fatherhood Initiative (www.fatherhood.org) provides the following advice on *What it Takes to be a Dad:*

☑ Read to your children.

☑ Keep your promises.

☑ Go for walks together.

☑ Let your child help with household projects.

☑ Spend time one-on-one with each child.

☑ Tell your children about your own childhood.

☑ Go to the zoo, museums, and ball games as a family.

☑ Set a good example.

☑ Use good manners.

☑ Help your children with their homework.

☑ Show your children lots of warmth and affection.

☑ Set clear, consistent limits.

☑ Consider how your decisions will affect your children.

☑ Listen to your children.

☑ Know your children's friends.

☑ Take your children to work.

☑ Open a savings account for college education.

☑ Resolve conflicts quickly.

☑ Take your children to your place of worship.

☑ Make a kite together.

But the real winners in a father/child relationship is the child, for without a father, children face overwhelming odds against living a productive life. Imagine your child as part of these Census Bureau statistics:

- 63% of youth suicides are from fatherless homes

- 90% of all homeless and runaway children are from fatherless homes

- 85% of all children that exhibit behavioral disorders come from fatherless homes

- 80% of rapists motivated with displaced anger come from father less homes

- 71% of all high school dropouts come from fatherless homes

- 70% of juveniles in state-operated institutions come from fatherless homes

- 85% of all youths sitting in prisons grew up in a fatherless home

- 70% of long term prison inmates come from fatherless homes

- Teen mothers are far more likely to have grown up in fatherless homes

Surprised? I was, especially when the role of a father has been traditionally limited to disciplinarian or banker. Common phrases from my childhood were, "Wait till your father gets home," and "Dad, I need some money."

Even today, many believe a father is incapable of nurturing a child. After all, how could a father understand what maternal instincts are? We don't carry the child for nine months.

But a man doesn't have to bear children to have the ability to nurture. The truth is that there is nothing a mother can do that a father can't. Okay, there is one thing, but that is why they sell formula.

The new challenges and adjustments that we face as single fathers can make us feel overwhelmed. Some single fathers encounter radical changes in their own personal behavior before finally adjusting to their new life. These may include depression, eating problems, sleep disorders, smoking, and drug or alcohol abuse. Some fathers will even develop stress-related illnesses such as back pains, headaches, heart attacks, common colds, and impotence. The best advice dealing with these issues comes from Dr. Whatwentwrong, "If you need help, get it. A father is absolutely no good to anyone if he is sick."

Mike, a custodial father of three, shares another common problem fathers face with divorce. "When my wife deserted us she made more money then I did. Our duel income supported two new cars, a home, and special care for my handicapped daughter. Now, without my ex's income and the reduced hours I am able to work, I have lost my home, my cars, and my savings."

These types of losses can certainly make adjusting to a single parent role more difficult. But it's not the end of the world. Mike has some sound advice for those in this situation: "Take a step back, regroup, and start over. Many successful people hit rock-bottom before reaching their goals. And there is nothing, except children, that can't be replaced. *(This includes the ex-wife.)*"

Realizing that no two situations are the same, we are all at one time or another bedfellows to loneliness, boredom, depression, anxiety, isolation, guilt, low self-esteem, and anger. When this happens it is important to overcome these negative feelings so you can live life to the fullest. There are no secrets and no short-cuts to doing this. It takes time, energy, and a positive attitude every day, starting today! Trust me, everyday then gets easier and more enjoyable.

The reality is that some fathers will have an easier time coping than others. Paul, a father who wanted his divorce and custody of his children says, "The start of my custody ended a volatile relationship and court battle. My first day of custody was a chance to start over and live peacefully with my kids." Fathers like Paul, who perceive the end of their relationship as a positive experience, will experience increased self-esteem, blooming maturity, and enhanced growth in personal relationships. And they'll probably wake up each morning with a hard-on, too.

However, fathers who did not want a divorce or custody may see their children as obstacles to getting laid. That's too bad, because these fathers will miss a lot of the rewards that go along with fatherhood, and adjustment to their new situation will be difficult.

The first step to a positive outlook is cutting the strings from the ex-wife and accepting that the relationship is over. For many, letting go is difficult. Some men hold onto unrealistic expectations and at times act stupidly. No doubt, breaking up is hard to do, but when ending a relationship is inevitable, make it as easy as possible for yourself by following these rules:

★   Don't act like a weak, quivering baby. Or at least don't let her see you acting like one.

★   Cut the strings! Leave her alone. Don't call, don't send cards, and never attempt to reconcile.

★   Accept that she is going to start a relationship that does not include you. And the sooner you get over it, the better.

★   Remember the not-so wonderful parts of your relationship and use these bad times as motivation.

★   *Get over it!*

★   Control your rage and jealousy. Don't stalk, harass, threaten, hit, grab, or touch her in any way.

★   Mind your own business. An ex-husband has no right to ask questions of his ex-wife, her friends, her co-workers, or her family. Besides, you won't like the answers anyway.

★   Do not break anything, *especially if it's yours.*

★   Leave her friends alone, especially her boyfriend. It's not his fault.

My father once said, "There is a fine line between love and hate, and in order to hate someone you must love them." My advice is, don't hate her. If a father is angry and consumed with the actions of his ex-wife, he will be unable to see the positive things in his life. Not only will he be unhappy, but it will be impossible to keep the best interests of his children in mind.

Letting go of the hate is just as important as letting go of the love and memories. For fathers struggling to let go, try some of the following. Force yourself if you have to:

- 👍 Laugh at something. Nothing heals like laughter.

- 👍 Stay close and rely on family and friends. They are the only ones willing to hear these kinds of problems.

- 👍 Begin a social life as soon as possible. A father needs to date and socialize to keep his sanity and to present a positive image to his children. They learn by example. Let them learn to be happy.

- 👍 Do something for yourself at least one day a week. Join a bowling league, exercise club, singles' club, or church group. Start a hobby or even return to school.

- 👍 Do something on a regular basis outside the home, and make sure it is *co-ed.*

- 👍 Buy something for yourself that will be seen often. I buy plants or something for our home. Clothes are a nice touch too.

- 👍 Buy a pet. Not just any pet, a dog. Not just any dog, a golden retriever. They are babe magnets.

- 👍 Call someone, but don't unload on them. With the exception of a close friend or family member, no one really wants to hear your problems. (You know, family and friends may not want to hear about them either!)

- 👍 Laugh at something. Nothing heals like laughter. (Just in case you missed this one before.)

👍 Go party a little. Attend a singles function.

👍 Make a new friend, or look up an old one.

👍 Try dating. There is nothing like replacing the old model with a new one.

👍 Pamper yourself. There is something about a bubble bath and a bottle of wine, especially when shared with someone.

👍 Spend some time alone and enjoy it.

👍 Consider hypnosis. Doctors often use hypnosis to help people stop smoking, lose weight, and overcome various phobias. It may be just the help you need.

👍 Take complete care of yourself. Just as physical health depends on a balanced diet for nourishment, mental and social needs also require nourishment. A single father is entitled to live a happy life. If not, he won't be of any use to anyone, including himself.

👍 Look to God, as faith can bring strength and inner peace. Spiritual health can contribute to a positive outlook on life.

👍 Avoid rushing into another relationship. Entering a relationship to make life easier, or because you need a physical relationship in your life, will fail. These reasons make for brief relationships and contribute to the 80 percent divorce rate for second-time marriages.

👍 Stop asking negative questions that deserve self-pity. If you ask, "Why me?" or "Why doesn't she love me?," your mind will find the answer, and you won't like it.

👍 Ask questions that result in positive actions or answers, such as, "What can I do to help myself adjust?" or "What can I do to improve my life?"

👍 Stop thinking of reconciliation. Any time this happens, hit your hand with a hammer until the desire is gone.

👍 Give yourself time to adjust. Tomorrow will be better, and before you know it, you're over it.

Make sure both you and your children are adjusting. Do not let depression last for a long period of time. If you need help, get it.

Go at your own pace, stay comfortable, and prepare for the fact that the first six months to a year are the hardest. Don't expect perfection from yourself or your children. If you make a mistake, try again.

The "Ex"

O h yeah, I almost forgot the ex-wife. Hard to imagine once feeling like a dog in heat over her, huh? *Funny how things change.* But let's begin this chapter of looking at the mother's role charitably, trying to see this new lifestyle from her perspective.

First, understand that society does not look favorably on the non-custodial mother, and she knows it. The first thought most people have about a mother without custody is the mother must be selfish, mentally ill, immoral, have a drug and alcohol problem, or be just plain emotionally unfit.

Peter shares his experience: "My daughter, Dawn, was in tears when she overheard her grandparents describe her mother as a whore with no morals. Dawn was depressed and mad at my mother and father for weeks."

The most unfortunate thing about these disapproving societal views is that they may have a negative effect on children's self-esteem. If this happens, try to stay positive about the ex-, their mother. If she is gone from their lives, present the circumstances of her leaving as a sacrifice on her part that was intended to benefit them. I know this will be hard for some fathers to do, but belittling a child's mother is detrimental. Children will feel it's wrong to love their mother and if you disgrace her, your children will suffer and possibly end up resenting you. If a mother is truly bad, her offspring will eventually learn it without anyone telling them.

Another problem may occur when a child idolizes the absent mother. In this case it is best not to counter such idealization, rather just let the child be. We all need our crutches.

A mother's feelings for herself may also be harsh and unforgiving. Don't believe for a moment that a mother could walk away from her children and never feel remorse, guilt, or shame. These are powerful emotions and can be difficult for some mothers to deal with, especially if Mom was unable to cope with the children or if she left for selfish reasons such as, "I need my space" or "I want to finish school."

These guilty feelings may result in mothers avoiding school functions and extra-curricular activities because these gatherings might expose the fact that they do not have custody. Some mothers may even have difficulty handling visitation. If the children are unloving or have hostility towards their mother, visitation is even more difficult. Some mothers find it easier to avoid these situations altogether which, unfortunately, can lead to total desertion.

On some level it may feel good not to deal with an ex-wife, but the other side of this is a terrible loss for the children. Having an active mother in their lives helps them adjust and accept their new life with fewer problems. Fathers also have assistance with child-care, transportation for school activities, support during sickness, and accommodation of personal time for things like sleep-overs. The bottom line is, keep the mother involved with the children. It's the right thing to do.

Unfortunately, this is sometimes difficult because many mothers have an abundance of unresolved anger left from the relationship or divorce which makes it easy to get into a shooting match of insults and rude behaviors. This hostility can make co-parenting extremely difficult. But it doesn't have to be that way. How does one break the habit of hurting each other? Kindness. Ohhhh! That's right, kindness! And dad goes first. Eeeeee! Start out slowly and use the telephone. Drop the sarcasm and say something nice, even if it is necessary to fake it. Showing concern for the children is usually a safe subject. Try telling her something that happened recently, like a new tooth. Inform her of a school activity or thank her for something like picking up the children. Don't worry, that nauseous feeling of being fake-nice will soon disappear, and she will volley her own compliment or kind action.

Over time, if she regresses to hostile behaviors, overlook them. Then, if at all possible, forgive her and continue with the kindness. Soon she will be unable to show hostility and be less likely to cause chaos.

If this fails, just ignore a nagging ex. Dr. Phil Stahl and Dr. Richard Mikesell describe "parallel parenting" for high-conflict situations as a parent in isolation from the other. Conflict is mostly reduced by decreasing exchanges of information and not always arriving at solutions.

A Father's Career

From the very first day of my new custody arrangement, there was no question that my job was important to our survival as a family. But what I didn't realize at first was the significance a career has on a man's sense of being a man. In childhood, we identify the traditional roles of men and women and correlate successful livelihood to manhood. Boys play construction while girls play house, and parents program us without thought. "I think Junior is going to be a doctor," says Mom. Some of us even grew up in homes where a mother's job was to stay home and care for the family, and how many of us have used "woman's work" as a demeaning cliché to elevate a man's work. No wonder we get obsessed with our careers.

Our ideas and opinions of male roles grew as we entered society and adapted to the traditional roles of a man: get a good job, work hard, and provide for the family. Our assessment of ourselves depends on our accomplishments and our ability to provide material goods. There's a bumper sticker that says it all: "He who dies with the most toys, wins."

In addition to society's pressures, men have peer pressures. Just like dogs sniffing each other's butts, we size each other's manhood by the importance of our job or the amount of money we make. "So Bob, what do you do for a living?" Come on, we don't really care what the other guy does, we just want to know if we do something better or make more money. It's a guy thing! Woof! Woof!

A successful career is so important to our existence that it often becomes our sole purpose in life and an escape from reality. We are fueled by the fix of recognition and money. We become consumed, sometimes to the point of ruining our health and losing sight of what is most important in life. Some of us are even guilty of being too busy for everyday parenting roles, and neglect our family.

For those of us who have been consumed by a career during marriage or prior to custody, this behavior cannot continue. A father must establish a balance among his job, himself, and his children. There must be time for parenting. A father should be able to occasionally have lunch with his children, attend a field trip, or come home early. If not, he is job-heavy and it is time he re-examined his priorities.

For some men, stepping back from a thriving career is difficult. After all, this has been our measure of success and what we feel most comfortable with. Yet, just as working too much can cause problems, so does being lazy. This condition is known as being butt-heavy, the opposite of job-heavy, but with a different set of problems brought on by a lack of money. To be successful in a career, one must show up for work on time, work everyday, and do more than what is asked.

Over the last 15 years I have seen this work ethic result in one promotion after another, including many of my own.

In order to provide a stable home for children, a father's career must stay on track, even if his home life is recovering from a train wreck. It's to be hoped that a *single father* won't experience difficulty maintaining or advancing in a career because of a new or different lifestyle. But it shouldn't be surprising if there is a career shift, position change, reduced hours, and worst of all, an income loss. The 1979 film *Kramer vs. Kramer* with Dustin Hoffman is still a chilling example of this.

In addition, some employers, knowingly or unknowingly, put ceilings on career advances until they are convinced that a father has adjusted to his new parenting role. And if that isn't bad enough, some fathers (including myself) are forced to refuse advancement because court orders prevent them from moving.

The good news is most employers are sensitive to the needs of their employees and are willing to adjust when possible. A father should immediately evaluate any added responsibilities he has and discuss them with management. For example, if a child visits an allergy doctor every week and relies on Dad to get there, Dad will have to schedule time off. Fathers also need to allow for school conferences, doctor visits, sick care, unexpected days off, and other interruptions. (With a little luck, not all on the same day!) Here are a few considerations that may help in adjusting to the added responsibilities of a *single father:*

- Consider part-time work or job sharing.
- Ask for flex-time. Not all employers are willing to provide this, but it is a nice way to maintain hours.
- Work a condensed week. Working four ten-hour days versus five eight-hour days may help.
- Take work home if possible. Many employers are only concerned with the completion of assignments, not actual hours in the office.
- If traveling outside of the office is necessary, carry a beeper or telephone. Always stay in contact in case of an emergency.
- Establish phone procedures with your children and employer for emergency and non-emergency calls.
- Discuss extra assignments with your employer such as overtime, travel, and entertainment, and plan ahead for them.

🍂 Don't take personal problems to work. Everyone has his
    or her own.

🍂 Make sure children understand work demands. Explain
    work so that they can understand the importance of
    keeping a job.

🍂 Take the first six to eight months into a new custody
    arrangement slowly, and do not grab too much extra
    work.

Maintaining a healthy career is an important factor in keeping
a positive outlook in life. My father once told me, "Don't keep
a job you don't like, or you will spend most of your life
unhappy." If a change in jobs is necessary, think twice before
quitting, **never** leave without giving proper notice, and be sure
to have a new job.

Co-Existing with
the Co-Parent

o-exist with my ex-wife? Share responsibility of the children's well-being? Develop a dialogue for discussing the children? Respect the rights and privacy of each other? Come on, the last time I looked, there was no "**X**" in cooperate.

When I think of my ex-wife, my emotions boil. I am constantly reminded of the anger and frustrations she caused me. The first thought that comes to mind is, "Why should I get along with her? I hate her."

I know now that is the wrong attitude for a father to have. But few of us control our feelings so readily. One does not have to like their ex to cooperate and be civil. This is a case of accepting our feelings, but changing our behavior.

Here is a response that appeared in Dear Abby where Judge Hass of Walker, Minnesota reflects on a case of extreme bitterness between two parents:

"Your children have come into this world because of the two of you. Perhaps you two made lousy choices as to who you decided to be the other parent. If that's so, that is your problem and your fault.

No matter what you think of the other party, or what your family thinks of the other party, those children are one half of each of you. Remember that, because every time you tell your child what an idiot his father is, or what a fool his mother is, or how bad the absent parent is, or what terrible things that person has done, you are telling the child that half of him is bad.

That is an unforgivable thing to do to a child. That's not love; it is possession. If you do that to your children, you will destroy them as surely as if you had cut them into pieces, because that is what you are doing to their emotions.

I sincerely hope you don't do that to your children. Think more about your children and less of yourself, and make yours a selfless kind of love, not foolish or selfish, or they will suffer."

I know this is a tough pill for some to swallow, but children with two parents have fewer problems growing up. The sooner parents find a way to cooperate, the sooner the children will become stable. And children aren't the only ones who benefit when parents cooperate. Dad is also a big winner. When a father can say, "I get along with my ex-wife," he has discovered confidence, maturity, and what it means to be an honorable man. In addition, having a mother involved helps lessen the load in the following situations:

- Assisting with school work.
- Shopping for clothes.
- Providing occasional child care needs. This is particularly helpful dealing with sick care, allowing time to travel, and providing well earned personal time at no expense.
- Discussing female "stuff" with a daughter.
- Being an emergency contact for day-cares and schools.
- Sharing transportation responsibilities.

So what can a father do when there is so much anger and hate that neither parent can get along? I wish I could develop a master plan for everyone to co-exist with his ex-wife, but that would be like prescribing a universal sexual position for mankind. The important thing to remember is not to stop trying.

I do have a suggestion for fathers who have difficulty finding a way to **start** a successful co-parenting arrangement. Try sending the following letter to your ex-wife. Assuming that both parents are adults who love their children enough to do what is right for them, this letter is a peace treaty in the form of a contract and is designed to provide the first step toward a peaceful relationship between hostile parents. Some people think living in harmony with an ex-wife is just a dream, especially if blinded by hurt and anger from a divorce. A very smart man once said, "If you think harmony can be achieved, it can. If you think peace will never happen, you're right again!" That man? Oh, that was me.

Dear _____:

Today I realized that our child(ren) is/are more important than we are, and it is time to co-exist on their behalf. With the forwarding of this letter, I offer peace and ask that we set aside our ill feelings and be civil to each other. I know there is anger and hate from past conflicts that may not heal for a long time, but if we do nothing to overcome these feelings *our children will suffer.*

I'm not asking for forgiveness, nor am I giving any. I am not taking or giving blame. I am simply asking that we wipe the slate clean and try to make tomorrow better, *for the children!* Perhaps, in time we can work out our differences, but in the meantime, we must not let them interfere with our being good parents.

You have my word. As of tomorrow my actions will reflect **my love for my children, not my hostility for you.** I will work at improving our relationship and keeping the children first and foremost in my life. I will make every effort to follow the rules of successful co-parenting and ask you to do the same. They are as follows:

- **I will not** blame you for a failed relationship or any other problem I/we have had.
- **I will not** argue and fight with you in front of the children.
- **I will not** speak badly of you to the children.
- **I will not** use you as a sitter.
- **I will not** discuss court disputes or adult problems with the children.
- **I will not** limit telephone access between you and the children.
- **I will not** use the children as spies.
- **I will not** send messages through the children.
- **I will not** make plans or arrangements directly with the children.
- **I will not** send money through the children.
- **I will** try to be on time and will call if I am late.
- **I will** send/return the children clean, fed, rested, and with clean clothes.

- *I will* be courteous and use words such as "thank you" and "please."
- *I will* communicate about the children's actions, developmental stages, adjustment, and well-being.
- *I will* try to agree on basic rules such as bedtime, TV, diet, discipline, etc.
- If I slip and make a mistake, *I will* try again tomorrow.

I Promise.

_____

Name

_____

Date

CHAPTER

7

Child Care

During the time I negotiated my custody arrangement with my ex-wife, I had concerns for the care my children would receive while I worked, traveled, and occasionally dated. How was I going to find affordable child care for my three sons, ages three, seven, and eleven? All of them had different day-care needs.

The first thing I figured out was that without quality child care I wouldn't have a social life or a career. I would be grounded. No one wants to go on a first date with a family of four, and I couldn't work and worry about my children.

As I started my search I found day-care centers, live-ins, nannies, in-home care, family care, baby-sitters, after-school programs, nurseries, pre-schools, co-ops, and more. There were so many choices I wondered how I would know which ones to use.

Most fathers in charge of child care have these multiple choices, and many of us wind up using a combination of care providers to meet our needs. Although each father has to decide what is right for him, decisions may be influenced by various factors:

- ◇ **Your income.** Someone making $25,000 a year will have a harder time finding affordable child care than someone making $50,000.

- ◇ **Your time frame.** Rushing a decision for child care can lead to a bad choice and a new search in six months. Finding a quality care provider is a lengthy process. Expect to be busy for a while.

- ◇ **The hours child care is needed.** There is only one thing that would have broken my spirits while I was searching for child care: if I had needed child care while I worked at night. My advice to a father working nights is get a different job!

- ◇ **Your values.** Some fathers will prefer to have children in a home environment or in a religious program. These preferences leave fewer choices.

◇ **Your demographics.** Someone living in a densely popu-
lated school district will have more choices than someone who lives in a rural area.

◇ **Your luck.** Some fathers will find ideal care providers
with little effort. Family members, the children's
mother, relatives, grandparents, or friends will appear
and offer their assistance.

What To Ask

I still remember my first interview with a care provider. Boy,
was it short! I had *no* idea what to ask. Over the next several
years, I developed a set of questions to help eliminate poor candidates.

The **first** question to ask is: **"Do you have space for my child
during the times I need it?"** If the answer is no, there is no need
to go further.

Continue with:

"What is the cost per day, week, or month?" I like to find out
up front if the fees are what I expected to pay. If they are not, I
have to ask if the child care arrangement justifies paying more
than planned. In addition, it is a good idea to compare prices of
at least three care providers. And don't forget, most of the time
you get what you pay for.

**"Will I be charged for missed days due to holidays, sickness,
visitation, and vacation?"** It is common for providers to charge
for sick days and other missed days, but don't be afraid to ask

them to reconsider this charge. Lay on the charm with statements like, "I would really like to use your services, but I'm a single father and will have difficulty making the necessary sacrifices to afford missed days." If they say there are no exceptions, yet they can provide the kind of child care desired, simply add, "But I guess your services are worth it." (Private or family care is more likely to negotiate pay schedules.)

"Do you deliver and pick up to and from school?" (if needed). This can be the difference between arriving for work on time or not.

"Are you an approved, registered, licensed, or certified care provider?" This is a sign that minimum standards are kept, not an indication of the quality of care provided. To assess quality of care thoroughly, a father must question and investigate every aspect of a facility.

"Are you equipped to care for any special needs my child might have?" Consider a child's health, diet, personality, behavior, or any other special needs they may have. Be up front. Don't spring a major detail on the care-giver after an agreement has been made. "Oh, I didn't tell you Junior is allergic to sugar?"

"Can you handle sick care?" Children get sick, and if they have siblings, they take turns. Plan for it! Yes, there are professional sick-care providers who would allow a father to work when children are sick, and sometimes this may be unavoidable; however, it is in the best interests of the children to stay home. This is the balance we discussed in Chapter 5.

"What is the adult-to-child ratio?" Watch for a provider who has more on the plate than can be eaten. The adult or staff to child ratio should fall close to these guidelines:

Age of Child	# of Adults	# of Children
Up To 2 Years	1	4
2 To 3 Years	1	6
3 To 4 Years	1	8
4 To 5 Years	1	12
5 To 10 Years	1	15
10 Years And Older	1	20

"What training and experience have you had in child care or education?" This is a sign of a committed care-giver; it shows who is just cutting grass and who is running a landscaping business. In addition, if there are other staff members, be sure to find out what their qualifications are.

"Are you and your staff trained in CPR and/or other emergency situations?" This is the difference between a baby-sitter and a true care provider.

"What activities are/will be planned?" Watch for lack of definite plans. A quality care provider will have indoor, outdoor, and off-property activities scheduled for the children.

"How do you discipline the children?" Give a specific example such as, "What would you do if two children were fighting over a toy?" Watch for excessive discipline or contradictory parenting styles.

"Are you insured?" Most state laws require that day-care facilities and their modes of transportation carry liability insurance.

"Could I have three names and telephone numbers of past and present customers whom I could call as a reference?" This can save a lot of time by weeding out problem care providers. Call the referrals and begin the conversation with a personal introduction. Then, state the purpose of the call and say that their answers will be kept confidential. Ask questions such as: **"How long did you use the services of the care-giver?" "What did you like and dislike?" "Why did you leave?" "Would you hire them again?"**

With these screening questions the selection process will be thorough and you'll have some idea of the care provided. Remember, don't hesitate to repeat questions and take notes. Now let's look at the choices.

Day-Care Centers

Day-care centers are baby-sitters away from home. They normally offer structured programs that include learning activities, recreation, and exercise. The children (as many as 40) are grouped by age and monitored by one or more adults. Most centers offer complete child care between the hours of 6 A.M. and 7 P.M. Services often include transportation to and from school, snacks, and some meals.

The advantages are that day-care centers offer professional, long-term, dependable, and educational child care. In addition, they are regulated by the state and maintain minimum safety and health standards.

The disadvantages are cost and increased risk of infectious illnesses. Outside of specialized care or nannies, day-care centers are among the most expensive types of child care. Also, as with all group settings, children are exposed to all types of illnesses. Locating day-care centers is as easy as picking up a phone book, driving to work, asking neighbors, schools and co-workers. One may also park in front of the neighborhood school during arrival or dismissal times and see who drops off and picks up children. Chances are, there are several centers that are convenient to work and home.

After locating a few centers, call and speak to the director, using the previous screening technique. If your questions are answered in a satisfactory manner then schedule a visit with your child during regular hours. Upon arrival, ask yourself, **"Does the center have a clean, well-kept look? Does it have an outdoor play area? Will I feel safe leaving my child here? Would I like to stay here?"** Next watch your child interact with the staff and ask yourself, **"Does the staff show genuine concern for my child, or are they just watching? Are the other children interested? Are there activity centers? Is everyone happy?"**

In addition to the screening questions, ask the following:

"What educational or professional training does the staff have?" Naturally, the more training the better.

"How long has the current staff been employed and how long have they been in the child care profession?" Watch for a high turnover or the possibility of unqualified staff members.

"How many full/part time employees do you have?" Each center may be different. However, it must still be able to provide care if someone is absent or on vacation. One final note. Day-care centers are a good source of occasional evening baby-sitters. Just ask.

Family Day-Care

Family day-care is child care in someone else's home, usually run by a mother which offers care for up to 12 children. This home can belong to a friend, relative, or neighbor. The advantages are a home setting, usually close by in a family neighborhood. In addition, in-home care may cost less, especially for more than one child.

The disadvantages are that some family care providers take vacations and alternate care must be found for that time. Also, some may not have the patience or training necessary to provide quality child care.

Locating in-home care-givers is as easy as asking for referrals from friends, co-workers, neighbors or schools, or driving by a neighborhood sign.

In addition to the screening questions ask the following:

"How long have you been a care provider?" Watch for the provider that says, "You are my first."

"How did you get started in child care?" Watch for answers that reflect no real interest in children or indicate that the service might be temporary.

"Who will watch the children if you are sick?" Many times other family members will fill in or participate in the child care business on an as-needed basis. Ask to meet them and find out what their level of involvement is.

"Is your house child-proofed?" Keep a special watch for a safe, clean home with a well-maintained play area. (See Chapter 10 to spot in-home hazards)

In-Home, Live-Ins, Nannies, Au-Pair, Housekeepers

In-home, live-ins, nannies, au-pair, and housekeepers are care providers in *your* home. In addition, many include some, if not all, domestic chores. They can be friends, relatives, neighborhood students, or professional nannies. Some arrive in the morning and leave in the evening, some work only after the children are out of school, while others live-in on a full-time basis.

The advantages are the reduced cost when paying for three or more children, and the individual care each child receives. This is especially helpful for children with medical problems or physical handicaps. Some live-ins will exchange or include living expenses in their salaries. In addition, having another adult in the house helps with sick care, prevents having to take small children or infants out in inclement weather, provides night-time care for that spontaneous date, allows more personal time in the morning, and accommodates irregular work and travel schedules.

The disadvantages begin with the loss of privacy. Finding personal time for intimacy is hard, and walking around the house in one's underwear is sometimes embarrassing. Some live-ins even share family functions, meals, and vacations. Cost can also be a disadvantage. Salaries for a professional nanny, or au-pair, may include room, board, workers' compensation, medical insurance, taxes, and paid vacations. However, some fathers manage this type of child care expense by offering less money when paying in cash. Often this can save both parties money.

Thomas A. Nicol, an attorney licensed to practice law in the State of Texas and experienced in these matters, warns that this type of activity is regulated by the IRS, federal law enforcement agencies, and state and local laws. All employers are responsible for payroll withholdings and tax reporting. If a father chooses to hire someone without knowing the rules, he could lose custody if the other side finds out and points out to the court (or immigration, the IRS, or anyone else) that dad is in violation of federal, state, or local laws.

Warning! This type of work attracts illegal aliens. Choosing this form of care is risky as many immigrants are unable to provide references, which makes it impossible to check out their past. In addition, many speak little or no English.

Locating in-home or live-in care is a little more difficult than the other forms of child care. Friends, relatives, and neighbors are always a good source, but one may also wish to include high schools, local colleges, churches, community centers, and local papers.

Caution! During the selection of students always check references and ask about their school activities. Look for someone well-rounded and polite.

In addition to the screening questions ask the following:

"Why did you leave your last position?" Watch for answers that are indecisive or reflect problems, and check references.

"How long do you see yourself working for me?" Be straight forward. You need to know if the candidate intends to be temporary or permanent. Remember, consistency is important to a child, and one certainly doesn't want to go through this process again in six months.

"Why do you want to be a full-time care provider?" You're looking for answers that reflect concern for the children and not someone just trying to make a buck.

"Can you drive?" "Do you have a car?" "Are you insured?" Individual needs may vary, but having someone to run errands is a big plus.

"Do you smoke?" Make sure you explain all the house rules.

"Do you have any special needs?" One may also wish to know personal information such as hobbies and commitments.

Pre-School and Nursery School

Pre-schools are child-care centers for children between the ages of three and five years. As the name implies, they are schools preceding kindergarten. Pre-schools are designed to be a transition between home and the start of actual school. Before enrolling there, children must be able to take care of themselves, such as using the toilet and dressing themselves. Children usually attend pre-school part-time, several hours a day, two to five times a week. Some schools are also connected to a day-care center and are capable of supplying necessary transportation.

The advantage is structured learning programs that focus on the development of a child's emotional, social, and intellectual skills. This is especially beneficial for a child who has been cared for at home and has not had the opportunity to develop many of the skills needed to enter the school system. This early educational start instills a positive learning attitude in children and gives them a learning advantage throughout their school years.

The disadvantages are cost and location. Expect fees to be slightly higher than day care and not always convenient to work and home.

Locating a pre-school is as easy as finding a day-care center. Because pre-schools must be licensed, they are listed with the Department of Human Resources.

In addition to the screening questions ask the following:

"Is there a registration fee?" Money, is there ever enough?

"How is my child's progress reported and monitored?" You will want regular progress reports and report cards.

"Are parents welcome without an appointment?" There should always be an open-door policy.

"How long has the staff been employed here?" Watch for high turnover.

"What formal training does the staff have?" Look for staff members trained in child care, health, and/or education.

Next, schedule a visit to the school during normal business hours with your child. Watch the children interact with the staff. The school should provide a happy, safe, and clean environment.

Before And After School Programs

Before and after school programs provide care for children attending first grade and up. Many times these programs are located in a child's own school gymnasium and offer structured programs that include quiet time for school work and activities for fun. Most operate after school and provide snacks. Some may also have morning hours and provide breakfast.

The advantage is convenient, low-cost child care for the few hours a child will be alone after school. (Mine was ¼ of what I paid for full-time care.) This gives dads extra time to get to work in the mornings as well as not rushing home to an unsupervised child. A benefit to the children is that they will most likely attend these programs with classmates, and will therefore adjust immediately.

The disadvantage is unqualified staff members. Not all employees are from the teaching or child care professions.

Locating one is as easy as calling your child's school, local YMCA, or community center.

Caution! Before enrolling a child in one of these programs, be sure to investigate the staff-to-child ratio, the staff's qualifications, the program activities planned, the mixture of children's ages, the condition of play equipment, and any transportation that might be provided. These programs are not affiliated with the school system. Do not assume anything!

Traditional baby-sitters (evening care)

Baby-sitters are care providers used for occasional, in-home, short-term (one to six hours) evening care. Most will also include some house work for a fee. Baby-sitters are usually local, female, high school or college students, and between the ages of 15 to 21. If they are available they will normally watch children with little notice, which is a good reason to hire girls with less active social calendars. It is helpful to locate at least three sitters you can call on.

The advantages are no long-term commitments, lower rates, and keeping children in their own beds at night.

The disadvantage is putting everything of value in the hands of a teenager.

Locating a baby-sitter is easy. Ask a friend, neighbor, relative, or anyone with children.

Caution! Realize that this is child care for a few hours. Don't expect to hire a registered care provider. Look for a mature, responsible person, and before turning one's worldly possessions over to a 15 year old, explain the house rules and established routines. Include information such as eating and sleeping habits for the children, policies for phone calls, visitors, smoking, eating, transportation, hours, and payment. It is also a good idea to talk to the sitter's parents and ask their permission and thoughts regarding their child's baby-sitting.

Before you leave for the evening, prepare your children. Stay positive and explain the evening's activities. Never give into whining. If you do it once, you'll pay the price even worse the next time. Before leaving, post all emergency numbers and always be available by phone or beeper.

One last thought on baby-sitters. *Don't even think about getting sexually involved with them!*

Baby-Sitting Co-Ops

Baby-sitting co-ops are made up of several neighborhood families who exchange occasional baby-sitting hours without money. The members are responsible for record-keeping and scheduling. Each time a member baby-sits a child, the sitter earns points. (Bonus points if meals are involved.) As one collects or *banks* points, they can draw from their account for exchange of child care.

These programs are okay for married couples, but not for a bachelor parent, especially if he has more than one child. A father of three could end up baby-sitting *Satan* for three nights to earn enough points to go out. Besides a single father does not have the time to baby-sit. Period!

Decision Time

Once you've determined what type of child care best fits your needs and interviewed appropriate candidates, it's decision time. Remember, the care provider must meet two objectives. First, the provider must offer a safe, loving, positive learning environment, and second, the provider must allow a father to feel comfortable at work by eliminating extra stress and worries.

Included in the selection process is finalizing all the arrangements and services. In almost all circumstances, a father will be asked to sign a contract or agreement. This contract is by no means non-negotiable and changes can be made providing both parties agree. But like I always say, "If you don't ask, they won't either."

Once a contract is signed, the father will also be responsible for providing the care provider with important current information including:

★   Two emergency contacts capable of making life or death decisions

★   Other persons authorized for pick-up

★   Any special instructions pertaining to a child's health, likes, and dislikes

★   Current immunization records

A father is also expected to show involvement in the care of his children and give respect to his care giver. This is as simple as asking relevant questions when dropping off and picking up children. Simply ask, "What is planned for today?" or "What did the children do today?" Besides being courteous this is also a great way to monitor a care provider. (It's actually the next best thing to talking to one's children.)

Respecting your care giver also means paying them on time. Imagine having to wait an extra week or more for a paycheck? But, if fees will be late, be honest and discuss payment with the care provider. Don't make them guess. And never ask a care provider to perform ***extra*** duties without offering some sort of compensation.

First Day

To prepare children for their new experience, take them on short visits to the care giver before the actual starting date. Make sure they are familiar with the restrooms, play areas, and other aspects of the center. It's also helpful if a father hangs around for 15 minutes for the first few days. When it is time to go, give Junior a hug and say good-bye. Do not sneak out, give into tears, or make a big deal out of saying good-bye. A child must accept and *expect* that Dad will leave and *return*. This way, when it is time for him to go on a date, the child will expect that, too.

When is change necessary?

If it is possible to keep a child in the same care at the start of custody, do so. It will make the other adjustments they go through that much easier. Changing care providers is some-times difficult for a child to understand. They often feel hurt or think they did something wrong. Some may even withdraw. This is a good reason why a father should try to work out minor problems with a care giver. Most will attempt to correct any known problem.

Although switching care providers should be avoided, a father must watch for signs that would warrant an immediate change. Some are:

- A child suddenly refusing to go to the provider
- A child experiencing a major behavior change
- A child showing signs of abuse and/or neglect
- A care giver that is unwilling to cooperate or who lies
- A care giver who has personal problems that conflict with individual family values

If changing child care is necessary, a father should stay positive and talk to his child about each day's events at the new provider. Be alert for any serious problems, but if the child only appears to be having trouble adjusting, make statements like: "Wow, that sounds like fun!" "I wish I could do that!" "What fun things do you think you will do tomorrow?" And it's always a good idea to have a replacement chosen should change become necessary.

Domestic Chores
Maid *Easy*

Within three days of my new custody arrangement, my house looked like a bomb had exploded in it. I had eight loads of dirty clothes, and "Dad, there's nothing to eat" echoed through the house.

I realized that day, if I were to survive, I would need to master *the big three*, cleaning (anything), washing clothes, and gathering food. And I mean **master.** I didn't just want to clean, I wanted to clean fast and know how to fit it into my busy schedule. I didn't just want to shop for groceries, I wanted to save money and know the best time of day to meet women. I didn't just want to toss my clothes in a machine, I wanted my $45 shirt to look good for three seasons. And I **never** wanted pink underwear!

Those were big dreams for a guy that knew nothing at all about domestic routine. Until then, my idea of cleaning the house was throwing out the dishes and vacuuming the carpet. *Doing the wash* meant dropping clothes off at the cleaners and grocery shopping was driving through McDonald's. Now that I think about it, I had the same opinion about painting my house. "Come-on, I've seen it done before! All you do is brush on some paint. How hard can it be?" Well, after I painted my house, I had my answer. It looked easy because everyone I watched knew exactly what they were doing. They knew the short-cuts, they had the right tools, and they had the know-how. I quickly drew the same conclusion about my household responsibilities and set out to tame the monster called "domestic chores." My greatest discoveries follow.

Pay Someone

The easiest way to keep up with domestic responsibilities is no secret, pay someone to do them. However, for most bachelor parents, having a maid is just a dream. Paying for help though, does not always mean paying someone to do everything. There are advantages to paying for just the services that one feels unqualified or unwilling to perform, such as home repairs or simple cleaning routines. I qualify my domestic expenditures by considering my budget restraints, peace of mind, and the extra time my decision gives me with my children.

For instance, in my house, making lunches in the morning is a difficult task. If I make them, my children complain and often won't eat. If I insist that my children make their own lunches, I must watch to make sure they contain more than just fats and sweets or I must yell so we're not late. This often puts me behind schedule and sends me to work upset, which is not the way I like to start the day. I would prefer to use the extra time to relax, clean the house, read a book, or prepare for work. For me, there is more value having my children buy their lunches rather than packing them. Each father has his own priorities. Some find spending $15 a week for dry-cleaning better than spending an hour or more ironing.

Another way to afford help is to barter. Occasional trades of labor can be as simple as cutting someone's grass in exchange for ironing shirts, or changing someone's oil in exchange for a couple hours of housework. The possibilities are endless. The secret is doing what comes easy to you and exchanging services that are demanding or time-consuming. I found there are generally people willing to exchange favors right next door. And if they happen to be single women, what an ice breaker! One last note on bartering as it relates to the law. The IRS requires reporting trades as income. Keep all records in a *safe* place or they might be forgotten at tax time. And wouldn't that be a shame.

Delegate

What if budget restraints do not allow luxuries such as a lawn service or a maid? Teach your children to help. Start at an early age and encourage them to pitch in. Explain how important their contribution is to the family. This will pay big dividends as they grow.

What are my children capable of doing? (My first question, too.) Here are some gender-free suggestions based on a child's age:

- **From the ages of three to five,** children are capable of simple chores such as picking up their toys (or trying to), making their bed, feeding pets, and putting away their clothes. This is a wonderful age to instill cooperation as children enjoy helping with everything. Use this time to teach, to praise, and to care for the development of your children.

- **From the ages of six to eight,** children are able to dress themselves, do school work, bathe, keep their rooms clean, set the table, water plants, make lunches, and take out the trash. At this age, it is important to encourage effort and expect them to complete each assigned task.

- **From the ages of nine to eleven,** children are capable of vacuuming, doing the dishes, cutting coupons, putting away groceries, and helping with meals. At this age, it is important to encourage responsibility by assigning chores on a weekly schedule.

🖐 **From the ages of twelve to sixteen,** children can babysit, do yard work, prepare food, wash clothes, clean windows, floors and bathrooms, help siblings with homework, and do more involved tasks such as washing the car or cleaning the garage. This is also the age they develop a social life and establish their independence, which makes it a perfect time to give them responsibility.

🖐 **From the ages of seventeen and up,** children, or should I say young adults, are capable of performing any household task. The difficulty at this age is that children, along with going to school and conducting an active social life, begin working at their own jobs. Some children must be strongly encouraged to help, or charged some type of rent. Set priorities and be firm, but fair. There are no free rides in life.

Remember, the most important parts of children performing chores successfully are the instructions and guidance they receive as they learn. Teach each chore as if the children are taking their first steps, and be careful not to overburden them. Outline each task with written or verbal directions, expectations, and time limits. Be patient and offer help when they need it. Focus on the completion of each task and praise them for a good effort. Then improve the quality of their work by making positive suggestions. Instill them with pride in everything they do. Eventually, children should perform their chores without being told, without supervision, and before watching TV.

To keep children motivated to do their chores, reward their efforts fairly. This can be done with enthusiastic praise or gifts, such as movies. Unfortunately, children move quickly from, "Look Dad, my room's clean!" to "Dad, how much do I get?" An allowance soon becomes a tool to motivate.

"An allowance? How much?" (I said that, too.) There is no set amount when it comes to giving an allowance and budget restraints can limit the amount, but too much generosity can give children the impression they live on easy street. If a weekly range is needed, try something close to this:

Under 5	$0
6 to 8	$2 to $5
9 to 11	$3 to $7
12 to 15	$5 to $15
16 and up	$10 to $25 (if the child is prevented from working outside the home)

There are other ways to give an allowance other than paying children a small amount of money. For example, give them a large amount and *demand* payment for their portion of rent, food, clothing, and utilities. This is a great way to teach them how to spend and budget money. If you treat them as adults when it comes to finances, they will be less likely to have money problems when they are grown. This idea is based on charging the child until enough money has been collected to cover the small amount they were going to earn anyway. Take warning, not charging accordingly can cost you some big money.

Learning give-and-take is their first step toward adulthood. (Okay, maybe pubic hair came first, but this one is really up there!) Following is a lesson plan on teaching finances to children:

- 💰 **Live on a budget.** Explain the difference between wants and needs. Children should understand how food, utilities, *cable,* emergency car repairs, sports fees, driver's education, or any other obligations effect spending.

- 💰 **Money doesn't grow on trees.** "Ahhh Dad, I didn't know you had to put money in to use this machine," my six year old said to me. Explain bank activities such as checks, ATMs, deposits, savings, interest, borrowing, and credit.

- 💰 **Save for tomorrow.** Every child should have a savings plan or at least a piggy bank. Instruct children to save at least 10 percent of their earnings.

- 💰 **Set goals.** Allow children to work toward a short term goal such as a video game or a special treat.

- 💰 **Be thrifty.** Children watch and learn from the spending habits they observe. If a father sets his priorities and makes sacrifices, children are more likely to do the same.

- 💰 **Know the value of money.** Although it is difficult to be happy and broke, remind children that money doesn't buy happiness and they should be thankful for what they have.

Be charitable. There is always a time for helping those who are less fortunate. Give a little.

Household Chores For A Lazy Man

As my domestic responsibilities increased, I searched for help. I read several books, women's magazines, and even called Mom a few times. Sure, I learned some interesting tips, like rubbing white bread on a lipstick stain, but I couldn't help thinking I wasn't any further ahead than when I started.

It wasn't that I needed to know how to clean a toilet. Household chores are not that difficult. Now don't get me wrong, I didn't say running a household is easy. Mastering the role of a domestic engineer is an exhausting, never-ending, thankless job. It requires balancing a career, running a household, raising children and having a healthy social life. It requires the one thing we all need more of: time.

One day, while hurrying to work, I discovered the secret to saving time and making household responsibilities more manageable. It was as simple as driving over a set of railroad tracks. Where is the connection? Consider how many people drive over a set of railroad tracks without really thinking about it. Most have no desire or cause to change their technique for such a routine procedure.

But what if one could save a few moments on that simple task? What if one could save a few more moments on another . . . and another? Time is saved in moments. These moments then turn into hours. All it takes is an open mind, common sense, and the answer to one simple question, "What can I do to make my job easier, faster, and better?"

In the case of driving over the tracks, an obvious answer is to move your car over 12 to 24 inches in either direction to avoid the rut that all the other drivers have caused. You wouldn't have to slow to a crawl before crossing, it would be easier on a car's suspension, and it would make traffic flow better.

Doing household responsibilities in the same manner can provide hundreds of time savers. It isn't *how* to clean a bath tub, it is *when*. The dirt is easier to remove after a shower. It isn't *how* to put away dishes, it's *where* to put them. It is easier for children to help themselves if glasses are on the lowest shelf. It is as simple as looking at things from a different perspective, like washing the floor when the children are at their mom's.

"If you want to learn an easier way to do things, follow a lazy man," my father used to say. I never thought of myself as lazy. Most men don't, but if easier is lazy, I'm okay with that. Here are some of my favorite time savers.

Morning routines are made easier by:

- 🌣 Doing as much as possible at night, like picking out clothes and preparing for work, before going to bed.

- 🌣 Staggering wake up times if there are not enough bathrooms.

- 🌣 Brushing your teeth and shaving in the shower.

- 🌣 Keeping a low maintenance appearance. Long hair and some facial hair require more time for grooming.

- Taking 15 minutes a day of undisturbed time for yourself. This time, either in the morning or just before bed, pays big dividends.

- Keeping all important numbers (schools, doctors, mother) posted near the phone. They'll be needed eventually, so plan for it.

- Keeping a coat rack or shelves near the door for backpacks, coats, gloves, and the like.

Kitchen duties can be made easier by:

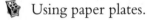 Making meals that can be prepared in one pan and in 30 minutes or less. (*See* Chapter 9 for fast, one pan recipes.)

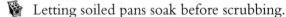 Cooking double portions and reheating leftovers.

Cleaning as you cook.

Using paper plates.

Letting soiled pans soak before scrubbing.

Organizing from a child's perspective. Children can help themselves if they can reach dishes, snacks, and other necessities. Stools can help here.

Using child-friendly products. Try snack-size containers, spray butter, individual toaster items, granola bars, and even sliced bread.

Bathrooms can be maintained more easily by:

 Using liquid soap.

Using toothpaste in a pump container.

Using color-coordinated towels and toothbrushes so you can find out who is leaving a mess.

 Using the week's worth of toothpaste that has built up in the sink to clean the chrome. That's right, after a rinse, toothpaste will leave fixtures sparkling.

 Using a mesh bag or container for bathtub toys.

 Using a cleaner made for bathrooms. There are several easy-to-use cleaners such as mildew removers, disinfectants, lime removers, and toilet bowel cleaners that clean, kill germs, and deodorize simultaneously.

General living areas can be maintained more easily by:

 Dusting from the top down, before vacuuming.

 Checking and fixing vacuum leaks, changing bags regularly, and keeping an extension cord on the vacuum that reaches everywhere.

 Reducing clutter. Avoid decorating with small knickknacks.

 Using throw rugs inside and outside of each entrance.

 Not smoking in the house.

 Purchasing a carpet cleaner. A dirty carpet can be a source of odors, not to mention how handy it is when there is two inches of water on your bathroom floor and someone yells, "Daddy, my Elmo got stuck in the toilet." A good carpet cleaner is worth its weight in gold. Children are constantly spilling and dropping things, and pets do much worse than that.

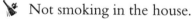

- Replacing furnace filters regularly.

- Collectively cleaning 10 minutes a day. Everyone working together can accomplish a lot in that short of time.

- Establishing a rule that everyone picks up his or her own mess and no one walks through the house empty handed.

- Using a squeegee to clean windows.

Children's rooms are maintained more easily by:

- Organizing from a child's perspective. Lowering coat racks, labeling drawers, and installing shelves and storage bins makes it easier for children to take responsibility for their own rooms.

- Keeping a laundry basket or hamper in each room.

Your room is maintained more easily by:

- Organizing everything. Keep a home filing system.

- Making your bed everyday. It brings a sense of self-worth and pride. My mother used to say, "A good man deserves to sleep in a made bed, and I ain't gonna make it for you." She had a point. Besides, it keeps the dust mites from landing on the pillow(s) and crawling into your brain.

Yard work can be made easier buy:

- Using gas tools.

🔪 Using a lawn mower with a wider cutting deck.

🔪 Planting low maintenance shrubs and using borders that are easily trimmed.

🔪 Pouring cement.

Laundry

The first rule of conquering laundry is reducing the amount of clothes that need cleaning. Start by wearing some clothes twice, even three times. If they are free of odor and stains, why not? Jeans, slacks, and anything that must be dry cleaned should be hung up immediately after wearing. A few days later, wear them again. The same goes for towels. There is no reason not to use them for five days or more if they are hung up after use. Another way to reduce the amount of clothes that need cleaning is to avoid buying clothes that require hand washing or must be washed separately.

Laundry: Begin washing clothes by sorting, selecting the right water temperature, and choosing the right detergent(s).

Whites, such as socks, underwear, light colored sheets, grays and towels should be washed in hot water with a cold water rinse. Use the longest cycle (8 to 12 minutes) and avoid overloading the machine. Overloading makes cleaning difficult and powdered detergents cannot dissolve.

For best results, use a name-brand, general-purpose detergent. I prefer one that has colorfast control, while some argue in favor of saving a few pennies with a generic brand. That is penny-wise and dollar-foolish. My clothes are clean, bright, and last longer because of the detergent I use. Ultimately, that saves money.

When washing whites, bleach is recommended for extra whitening and disinfecting. However, be careful not to use more then one cup for a regular load. Too much will destroy the fibers in clothes and lead to premature wear. If bleach is added to the machine through the automatic dispenser, be sure to rinse the dispenser and surrounding areas with water. One stray drop of bleach can ruin a $35 pair of jeans. And never pour bleach directly on dry clothes. Wait until the machine is full of water and running.

The dryer should be on the regular or permanent press cycle. Although most dryers have a cool down period at the end of the cycle, it is best not to allow dry clothes to sit in the dryer as this will leave wrinkles. Drying should also include a dryer sheet to remove static cling and make the clothes (and house) smell fresh. I prefer cost-effective, generic brands and use them several times before throwing them out.

Permanent press clothes, such as colored T-shirts, jeans, shorts, and everyday clothes, should be washed in cold (or warm) water for four to eight minutes with a cold water rinse. Also consider turning clothes inside out. Who cares about wear on the inside of a colred shirt? But it'll be noticeable on the outside. If there are several loads to wash, sort these clothes by fabric, color, and the amount of dirt. Wash heavily soiled clothes separately.

Dry these clothes on the permanent press cycle with a dryer sheet and avoid drying thoroughly. (This is the number one cause of wear.) Instead, dry the clothes halfway, then put them on hangers to finish drying. This is a good way to reduce wrinkles, prolong the life of the clothing, and cut energy costs. I find it easier to run a load of clothes at night and dry them halfway (excluding delicate clothes). Then, in the morning, before I jump in the shower, I turn the dryer on. Twenty to thirty minutes later I fold and put them away. One load takes about five minutes of actual work.

Delicate clothes such as dress shirts, concert shirts, team jerseys with iron on letters, dress pants, anything with embroidered logos, and anything worth the money paid for it should be washed and rinsed in cold water with a mild detergent such as *Woolite*. Use the delicate or short permanent press setting. It is also important to sort these clothes by color and remove them from the washer and dryer immediately. If a light colored shirt is washed with a dark one, don't be surprised if one turns gray.

The life of these clothes can be extended by avoiding the dryer. Hang lightweight T-shirts and slacks that won't show stretch marks when hung to dry. Anything heavy should be laid flat to dry to avoid stretch marks. If drying is necessary, use the delicate or air fluff setting and dry only for a short time. Then hang or lay the clothes flat while they are still damp.

For those who decide to wait and wash several loads in one day, start with a load of whites. They are the easiest to find and take the longest to wash and dry. Once they are in the wash, finish sorting and pre-treating the rest of the clothes. After the white clothes are in the dryer, wash a load of delicate clothes. This load will finish before the white clothes are out of the dryer.

Hang as many delicate clothes as possible without drying. Start the next load of clothes, and by the time they are done, the whites will be dry and ready to be folded. Put any clothes remaining from the delicate load in the dryer and start folding the whites. By the time they are folded, the delicate clothes are ready to be hung and the third load from the washer is almost ready to be put in the dryer.

If there are more clothes to wash, get started. Rotate loads by drying times. Wash one load that requires long or full drying, such as denim, then wash a load of clothes that dry in a short time, such as shirts.

When trips to a laundromat are necessary, sort and pre-treat the clothes at home, and don't lug around large containers of bleach and detergent. Pour off small measures into containers that are easy to carry. Upon arriving, start a load of whites immediately. They take the longest to dry and must be completely dry before folding. Once they are washing, start the other clothes in this order: jeans or denim, towels, permanent press, and delicate. The delicate clothes have the shortest cycle. When they are finished, put them in the dryer. The other clothes will be finished and ready for the dryer soon. In a short time the (half dry) delicate clothes will be ready to be hung and part of the wash is complete. This also means there is a dryer open with time left on it. Either transfer some heavier clothes (jeans or towels) to the now available space, or use it to dry one of the lighter loads. Next, hang the permanent press;

the jeans will be ready soon, followed by towels and whites. Try to hang as many clothes as possible while they are still damp.

In Chapter 16 there are several ways to meet women, but talking about laundromats wouldn't be complete without touching on that topic now. After all, opportunity is half of the battle. And the opportunities increase when visiting laundromats during the evenings and weekends. Avoid Monday through Friday during normal business hours. The only women washing clothes at this time are housewives.

Meeting a woman at a laundromat is fairly easy because the conditions produce an innocent or coincidental meeting. Women are less likely to think, "he is just there to pick someone up." Also, most women know that there is a good chance a man is single by the simple fact that he is alone in a laundromat. No ring on the finger is another good sign.

Just as a man can tell if a women is available by the clothes she is hanging (men's work uniforms are a bad sign), women can tell a lot about a man in the same way. Take warning. Don't say, "I'm a pilot" if hanging uniforms from Joe's Garage.

Stains: The best way to deal with stains is to prevent them. However the truth is, children will spill, slide, and soil their clothes. The secret to removing stains is getting to them fast. The longer the stain is on the clothes, the harder it is to remove. So treat the spot right after it happens. I remove 99% of stains with a pre-treatment such as *Shout* or *Spray 'n Wash.* They are fast, easy to use, and work. (There are also travel size packages that allow for fast treatment of stains.) Just spray the stain, let it sit for a while, and wash. Liquid detergent works too. After the wash cycle, check to see if the stain is gone. If it is not, spray it again, let it soak for an additional twenty minutes then wash it in a higher water temperature. Do not dry clothes with stains in them as this often sets the spot into the fabric, making it impossible to get out.

Ironing: The best way to deal with ironing is to reduce the amount of clothes that need it. This can easily be done by buying permanent press clothes, drying them as discussed above, and hanging them immediately after removing them from the dryer. It also helps if clothes go to the cleaners occasionally. After professional cleaning, clothes hold creases for several washes and ironing is much easier. This is especially helpful with jeans and pants. New jeans should be taken to the cleaners before wearing them for the first time. This creates a natural crease that will wear into the character of the denim.

If ironing is necessary, follow the recommended temperature setting listed on the garment's care tag. This is important because it is easy to damage clothing with too much heat. Of equal importance is caring for the iron. They are not designed to go over zippers or buttons and should be cleaned occasionally, simply by ironing a damp towel. Steam jets should be cleaned annually by pouring a small amount of white vinegar into the water chamber followed by a water rinse.

Shirts: For best results spray lightly with starch and iron while damp. If the starch turns white, you are applying too much or your temperature setting is too high. Start ironing with the collar, cuffs, and sleeves, and then use the square end of the ironing board and finish the body of the shirt. Back first, then the front.

Pants: Begin by turning the pants inside out and ironing the pockets if needed. Then, reverse and iron the outside pocket area. Next, lay the pants flat on the ironing board and align the creases. Fold the top leg back and iron the bottom leg. Then unfold the top leg to the original position and iron it. Finish by turning the pants over and repeating the last two steps.

Gathering Food

Let's start grocery shopping with the best time of the day to go. If convenience, easy access, and short lines are a priority, try shopping early in the morning, late at night, or during normal business hours Monday through Friday. Avoid weekends. If freshness and selection are top on your list, try shopping early in the mornings, especially Saturday. If meeting women is a priority, try after work or early evenings. Avoid mornings during the week.

Next, let's decide where to shop. Look around at the choices of stores and evaluate more than the distance from home. Start with the store's location. Is the neighborhood rich, poor, new, or old? Stores that are in lower income areas are more likely to make low prices a priority. Unfortunately, this is often a trade off for quality. If you want to up your chances of meeting women shop at stores near apartments. And if price is not a priority, shop at a new store. They are nice, well lit, clean, and the clientele is normally up-scale.

When I first started shopping, I underestimated the chore of bringing home food. "No big deal," I said. "They must have a system in there. Don't they?" In just a few visits I realized there are no rules and that people have no manners. It's everyone for themselves. Shoppers maneuver their carts and go about their business the same way they drive over the railroad tracks, without regard. So, I have developed 10 commandments for grocery shopping.

1. Thou shalt be prepared to pay.

2. Thou shalt not block the aisles with thy cart or body.

3. Thou shalt not block the entrance and exit doors.

4. Thou shalt not eat food from the cart or shelves.

5. Thou shalt not forget there are other shoppers.

6. Thou shalt not use the express checkouts with too many items.

7. Thou shalt not park a grocery cart against the meat counters and block the way of others. (This is the only place in the store where it is acceptable to park a cart in the middle of the aisle.)

8. Thou shalt not let children run loose in the store.

9. Thou shalt not leave frozen foods (or trash) on the shelf just because "I changed my mind."

10. Thou shalt not let shopping carts go loose in the parking lot.

Before beginning your shopping, understand that no store is set up for convenience. That's why they put the milk at the back of the store. The owners believe if people must walk by hundreds of other products, they will buy something else. This unconventional way of arranging things means starting at one end of the store and finishing at the other, and will produce melted frozen items and mashed bread. The best way to maneuver through the store begins with health products such as shampoo, aspirin, and beauty aids. Then continue with household items such as detergents, cleaners, and paper products. Next, shop for canned foods, baking supplies, cereal, and drinks. These items are not perishable and will not be crushed by putting other products on top of them. After that, select refrigerated or frozen items, followed by meats, fruits, vegetables, and bread. Finally, head for the checkout counter. As you unload the groceries, try to put the heaviest items first. Do not trust the clerk to know how to bag groceries without smashing them.

Gathering for less: Saving money on groceries is essential. The money saved can equal a date, an oil change, a round of golf, or a pair of shoes. However, finding the best deal means knowing how much items cost and what is the best buy. The following quiz is designed to measure the shopping *cents* of both the novice and advanced shopper.

1) Store number 1 has a box of cereal (20 oz.) advertised for $2.89. Store number 2 has the same product for $2.50. Which store is cheaper?
   a) Store number 1.
   b) Store number 2.
   c) They are the same.
   d) Store number 3.

The answer is b. If you selected any other answer, do not shop alone. This is the first way to compare prices and decide the best place to shop. Start by shopping at one store and become familiar with the prices of at least 15 to 20 items. The more remembered or written down, the more saved. (I never thought I would see the day I could not remember a spark plug gap, but knew the price of pancake mix in three different stores!) When comparing these items use a mix of popular items that are normally priced the same each week, such as orange juice, milk, and bread, along with expensive items such as laundry detergent, pet food, and trash bags. Use caution when pricing fruits and vegetables. These prices rise and fall weekly due to weather, transportation costs, and crop size.

2) There is a 12-pack of your favorite beer for $8.59. Next to that is the same beer for $3.49 a six pack. What do you do?
   a) Buy the 12 pack and go home.
   b) Buy two (or more) six packs and go home.
   c) Report the cost difference to the first employee you see.
   d) Take advantage of the sale by buying all they have.

The answer is b. This is a typical example of larger quantities not always being cheaper and the importance of comparing prices of different sizes.

3) There is a 12-pack (12 oz. cans) of Pepsi for $3.99, and a 2-liter bottle (66.6 oz.) of the same for $1.25. What size should be used to calculate unit cost?

a) 12 pack
b) Liter
c) Ounce
d) Each

The answer is c. Here there are multiple sizes at different prices. The only way to compare prices and determine the best buy is by unit price. The unit is determined by a shared packaging size such as ounces, cups, weight, or each. The good thing about unit pricing is some stores use labels that list unit price along with the item cost. This makes the decision process easy. Other stores provide a calculator on the cart for your convenience.

With the following information, answer the next three questions. A box of 10 (net weight 12.3oz./350g.) Homestyle Eggo waffles cost $2.30, and a family pack of 16 (net weight 1lb. 3.8oz./560g.) cost $2.72.

4) Which is the better buy per unit? (And don't do your math here.)
   a) The box of eight
   b) The family pack
   c) There is no difference in cost
   d) I don't eat Eggos

5) By how much?
   a) $.50
   b) About half
   c) 4
   d) $.06

6) How much do you save if you buy the box with the cheaper unit cost?

    a) $.24

    b) $.06

    c) $.96

    d) $.50

The answers for 4, 5, and 6, are b, d, and d. The difference is calculated by dividing the cost by the unit size for each package, and then subtracting the two answers. In this case, $2.30 divided by 10 = $.23 each. The family pack is calculated the same way, $2.72 divided by 16 = $.17 each. That is a difference of six cents for each waffle and the savings of 6 cents on 16 waffles, or a total savings of $.96.

7) Kraft has an 8 oz. (2 cups/227g.) bag of shredded cheese for $2.09. Sargento has a 12 oz. (2.4 cups/318g.) for $3.36. Which is the best buy?

    a) Kraft

    b) Sargento

    c) Can't compare different manufactures

    d) Can't compare different sizes

The answer is a. This is an example of different packaging making price comparisons a little more difficult. Larger quantities can be deceiving because they are not always cheaper.

And there are more ways to save money on groceries other than price comparisons. Try some of these:

- **Use a grocery list.** This is a good way to speed up the visit to the store and avoid return trips for forgotten items. Keep a working list in a visible place (on the refrigerator) during the week. When it is time to shop, a quick look around will complete it.

- **Avoid impulse buying.** Grocery stores will try to *hook* customers into purchasing more expensive items by placing them at eye level. Finding a good deal is as simple as looking on the top shelf. Also, avoid items at the end of the aisle. These are put there for impulse buying and are not always the best price. The same holds true with items marked as "specials." They are not always the best buys.

- **Use coupons.** If it is possible, shop where they double and triple coupons. However, use coupons with caution. Some items, even purchased with a coupon, can be priced higher than a competitor's regular price. And coupons are easier to use if they are organized in an index box or accordian made for them.

- **Shop in a store that honors any advertised price.** This is a great way to save money. Save the grocery flyers that arrive during the week or are in the weekend paper, and circle the items that you will purchase. All stores advertise loss leaders to bring customers into their store, so this is a great way to take advantage of them all in one place.

- **Eat before shopping.** A full stomach is less likely to buy on impulse and purchase unnecessary items.

Buy fruits and vegetables when they are in season. Don't buy nectarines in the winter when they are $1.89 a pound. Wait until they are in season and their price is about $.99 a pound.

Read store ads and plan the week's meals around them. Looking at flyers from one store: A ten-pound bag of potatoes sells for $1.89, six ears of corn for $1.00, and whole chickens for $.59 cents a pound. For my family of four, that equals a dinner with leftovers for about $7.00.

Set aside a small amount of money for power buying. This should include taking advantage of sales and buying larger, more economical sizes from warehouse or discount food stores. If some quantities are too big, ask a neighbor or friend to split the purchase.

Buy generic if possible. While quality varies, some generic products are made at the same plants that make name brands. There are some items such as bleach and aspirin that must contain certain items to be called what they are. Aspirin is aspirin, bleach is bleach.

Shop at day-old stores. The food is still fresh and the prices are lower.

Watch the clerk. Don't expect the kid with the funny haircut and pierced nose to be perfect. Try to remember the prices of the articles purchased. If they don't ring up the correct price, say something.

Fast and Easy . . . Meals

When I assumed custody of my children, I was a heat and reheat cook. I thought, "What's the big deal? The instructions are on every package." Today, I can cook more than 100 dishes. Why did I change? I met Gena. A 26-year-old gymnast who was, flexible, but that's another story.

For a whole season of little league baseball, I sat behind Gena trying to find out her dating eligibility and learn more about her. One day, I overheard Gena tell her girl friend she preferred to date men who were good cooks. She said, "If a man is capable in the kitchen, he is capable in bed." And all this time I thought, "You can cook?" meant exactly that. Turns out it really meant "You're good in bed?" Knowing I would eventually ask Gena to dinner, I thought I'd better brush up on my cooking skills or I might never make it to the bedroom.

Cookbooks

My first stop on the journey to culinary bliss was not in the kitchen, but in a bookstore to buy a cookbook. There are hundreds to choose from, ranging from ethnic preferences such as Mexican and Italian, to health preferences (lowering cholesterol, vegetarian dishes), to cooking with crock pots, woks, and more. I suggest everyone have at least one cookbook, but I must admit, now that I have an established menu plan, I only refer to it when Gena visits.

Selecting a cookbook is as easy as picking one up and looking through 20 to 40 pages. If there are three to ten recipes of interest, chances are the book will do.

Personally, I like cookbooks with a photo of the finished dish for the same reason I like to see a picture of a complete puzzle before I put it together. I want to know what it *should* look like. Another advantage of a photo is screening a child's taste before cooking. Simply show the photo to your child and ask, "Does this look good?" I was disappointed when I served a perfect trout amandine and my children said, "I'm not eating this stuff."

Photos also encourage children to be involved with kitchen responsibilities: "This looks good. Let's make it!" Like my mother says, "A child's independence starts at home, and there is nothing wrong with beginning in the kitchen."

Cookbooks are also good sources for entertaining tips, menu planning, nutrition recommendations, table settings, and more. Think of them as a *Chilton's Manual* for the kitchen.

Now, I must confess, I thought using a cookbook in front of Gena would make me look bad. That would be like having to read the instructions on a condom during sex. So, I decided to memorize a couple of recipes. Good thing I did, as I discovered many valuable unwritten lessons.

First, I found recipes to be like directions found in a child's toy. Everyone knows that's just a suggested way to put it together. And just like putting children's toys together, mistakes can be made when one drifts too far from the recommendations. The only difference is, one can't return a T-bone steak with, "Excuse me, I'd like to exchange this for one that doesn't have mushroom sauce on it." Still, I believe one shouldn't be afraid to season to taste, to substitute or delete ingredients, or to combine recipes. This isn't Chemistry. It's Home-Ec.

Another lesson I actually learned while I was in the ninth grade. "Always read the entire test before starting," Mr. Ronald would say. What a waste of time, I thought. Then came the final exam. After working feverishly to complete the test, I reached the last the question. It read, "Education is not limited to the lessons we learn from books, and success cannot always be measured by a test score. Today, I hope you learn something. Answer only the first question."

Recipes are sometimes written the same way. They list the ingredients, and right after you put them together, the recipe reads, "Add the remaining ingredients (except the oregano) ten minutes before serving." Reading the recipe first also allows for preparation time and gathering the ingredients, avoiding that last minute trip to the store for dill weed.

Spices

Next, I thought an experienced chef should have a collection of spices. So, I bought everything. Even a spice called cumin. I figured with a name like that, how could I go wrong? Big mistake. I wasted a lot of money, and I still don't know what the hell *saffron* is. Now I use 40 easy menu selections (found in this chapter) that share the following ingredients:

Salt	Pepper
Powdered sugar	Sugar
Basil	Oil
Garlic powder/salt	Vinegar
Bullion, beef/chicken	Oregano
Olive oil	Shortening
Red wine vinegar	Cinnamon
Fiesta fajita seasoning	Paprika
Bread crumbs	Vanilla

Cookware

My first recipe called for a two-quart saucepan and a deep-frying pan. When I looked at my pots and pans I said, "I can't cook with this mess. Gena will know I don't cook." So, off to the store I went for new cookware. There are so many choices. I didn't know what was good, what was bad, why some were cheap, or why some were expensive. I stood with amazement at the vast assortment before my eyes. "What do I need?" I asked the sales woman.

She started with, "That depends."

Here are a few points to consider when deciding on what cookware to buy:

Cost: Prices on pots and pans can range from $50 for a set to $200 or more individually. I have burned food in both cheap and expensive pans. My advice is to buy the cheap ones and care for them.

Clean-up: Nonstick coatings make clean up a breeze. However, once the coating is damaged from using metal utensils or from improper storage, the pan quickly loses its easy cleaning feature and the pan must be replaced.

Construction of the handle(s): Wood is nice to look at, but is not recommended for the dishwasher. Metal gets hot, but can be used in an oven. And plastic is dishwasher safe, but will melt in the oven at high temperatures.

Heat distribution: The best is copper, followed by cast aluminum, stainless steel, enameled cast iron, and glass. (Cost normally follows the same order.)

Serving size: The number of servings can impact one's decision, but allowing for left overs, I have narrowed the choices down to the following:

Must Have

- 👍 1-quart saucepan with lid
- 👍 2-quart saucepan with lid
- 👍 4-quart saucepan with lid
- 👍 2 non-stick frying pans with lids
  (10" to 12", deep sides, oven safe)
- 👍 Casserole dish
- 👍 9" x 12" glass baking dish
- 👍 Pizza pan
- 👍 Cookie sheet

Nice To Have

- ☞ 6 to 10 quart stock pot
- ☞ Meat-loaf pan
- ☞ Steamer
- ☞ Roasting pan
- ☞ Tortilla pan
- ☞ 10" x 14" glass baking dish
- ☞ 6" non-stick frying pan with lid
- ☞ Extra and double of everything

Cooking Utensils

A kitchen without cooking utensils is like a mechanic without tools and it is a dead giveaway of a novice cook. Ask a mechanic, "What tools do I need?" and he can recommend what is essential and what is nice to have. This is what's in my kitchen tool box:

Must Have

- Measuring cups and spoons
- Plastic spatula (for pancakes)
- Rubber spatula (for scraping)
- Colander (strainer)
- Ladle
- Serving spoon
- 10" Chef's knife
- Paring knife
- Vegetable peeler
- Cutting board
- Bottle opener
- Can opener
- Meat thermometer

Nice To Have

- Cheese Grater
- Pepper mill

☞ Barbecue tools

☞ Tongs

☞ Basting brush

☞ Slotted spoon

☞ Rolling pin

☞ Knife set

☞ Pot holders

☞ Wooden spoon

☞ Garlic press

☞ Potato masher

☞ Oven thermometer

Appliances

It wasn't long before I saw modern appliances as love tools of the kitchen. Here are my favorites and their benefits:

Microwave: Corn on the cob (in the husk) in six minutes, baked potato in four to six minutes, leftovers in two to four minutes. Microwaves are a must.

Toaster/Roaster-oven: These are great for preparing leftovers and single portions without wasting time, energy, and money heating a conventional oven. They save counter space if hung from under a cabinet and can handle thick slices of bread and bagels. Oh yeah, they make toast, too.

Toaster: Just make sure it holds at least four slices.

Coffee pot: Some of us can't live without one.

Blender/Mixer: In addition to frozen drinks, blenders are great for making milkshakes and fruit drinks. I also use mine to puree recipe items, such as onions and mushrooms, that don't appeal to children.

Hand mixer: These are great when mixing mashed potatoes, burgers, meat-loaf, pancake batter, pudding, whipped-cream, and cake mixes.

Electric can opener: In our open-heat-and-serve society, these are faster than hand openers, and children can use them.

Crock pot: These are great for one-pan meals. Toss in the ingredients in the morning. When you arrive home, dinner is ready.

Bread machine: These are great for making pizza dough, and various bread products. They are fully automatic and can be programmed to have bread ready before your alarm goes off. What a way to start the day!

Food processor: This is a toss up. It takes me just as long to dice an onion by hand as it does to take my food processor out, use it, wash it, dry it, and put it away.

Outdoor gas grill: For me, this is a must. Grills require little maintenance (burn it, and scrape it with a wire brush), they make food taste better, they keep the heat outside, and grilling is better than frying food in oil.

Waffle maker: I have two. One for regular waffles and one for Belgian waffles. The Belgian waffles win, hands down.

Food dehydrator: I don't think I would have purchased this product on my own, but that would have been my loss.

Dehydrators are great for making both turkey and beef jerky; healthy fruit snacks such as dried bananas, apples, pears, and watermelon; drying spices and vegetables; and almost anything else that will fit. This is the most fun one can have in the kitchen with your clothes on.

There are other appliances to consider such as pasta makers, steamers, juicers, espresso machines, coffee grinders, woks, electric frying pans, rotisseries and more. My advice is, if it saves time, use it.

Tableware

My kitchen was almost complete. The only thing left was tableware. After all, I could not serve Gena from a Mickey Mouse plate and a jelly jar. Here are my suggestions for in-home dinning:

- 8 or more drinking glasses, buy a set; they're cheap.

- 4 wine glasses, better than making a toast with plastic cups.

- 4 to 8 place settings, plates, bowls, saucers, coffee cups, dessert plates, buy a set; they're cheap, too.

- 2 sets of matching silverware, and yes, there will still be times there are no spoons.

- 4 to 8 steak knives.

- 2 serving bowls, plain in color or clear to match anything.

- Salt and pepper shaker.

One last note on setting up a kitchen. Don't expect to make all your purchases at once. That would be quite an expense. These items can be found at most garage sales or pawn shops at a fraction of the cost. (You might also be surprised who you might meet there!) Tableware may also be purchased at reasonable prices from discount department stores.

Food Facts

I was excited when I discovered how to use food in the pursuit of love. Who would have thought that cucumbers, bananas, or other phallic-shaped food can actually make someone think of sex (no more tacos!), or eating celery can attract women like a pheromone spray. That's right, experts say, celery contains androsterone, a potent male hormone that attracts women. This androsterone is released (undetected) through perspiration (after eating, don't carry it in your pocket) and transforms Joe Average into Joe Stud. Surely, with such knowledge Gena would be putty in my hands. And that's not all. Here are some other love foods:

 Eating zinc-rich foods such as crab, eggs, garlic, milk, mushrooms, oatmeal, oysters, pork, pumpkin seeds, sunflower seeds, and spinach produces testosterone, a sex drive hormone.

 Drinking coffee may provide more than just a caffeine buzz. It is said that people who drink one cup of coffee a day are more likely to be sexually active than those

who don't, and men who drink coffee are less likely to
have problems with erections.

 Eating chocolate releases a chemical called phenylethy-
lamine, said to raise blood pressure and heart rate, creating the sensations associated with arousal.

 Drinking alcohol will loosen inhibitions and boost
testosterone. But be careful, after three drinks it
becomes more difficult to become aroused, and chronic
users have lower libidos than occasional drinkers due to
decreased testosterone levels. Likewise for women. A
few drinks can cause them to drop their defenses, but
too many can lessen their pleasure.

 Whipped-cream. For some reason, it just makes one
think of sex.

 Eating can be a turn-on too. Try feeding your partner a
sweet dessert or sampling food from her finger.

Safe Food

Contrary to this great knowledge of love food, I was disappointed when I learned that improper handling of raw meat,
chicken, eggs, and shellfish can spread salmonella, e-coli, and
hepatitis, causing illness or death. I don't know, call me sick, but
all I could think of was sending the kids to Mom's, seducing
Gena with a candlelight dinner, and then having her puke during sex. Follow these guidelines for safe food:

Clean everything. Use an antibacterial cleaner/soap (or bleach and water) to clean counter tops, cooking utensils, refrigerator surfaces, and hands. Be especially careful with cutting boards. These should be cleaned with disposable paper towels to avoid transferring bacteria to other surfaces. In addition, don't chop vegetables or salad ingredients with the same knife and cutting board used for raw meat, poultry, and fish. And don't use the same platter to serve cooked meat that was used to carry it to the grill.

Wash all fruit and vegetables with cold water before eating.

Keep cold food cold. Keep the refrigerator below 40 degrees Fahrenheit and the freezer at 0 degrees to prevent the growth of bacteria. And never thaw or leave refrigerated food at room temperature. Bacteria will flourish at room temperatures.

Keep hot food hot. Keep food at serving temperatures until served, and refrigerate leftovers within two hours to prevent the growth of bacteria. Never leave food at room temperature.

Do not eat raw eggs. This includes eating uncooked recipes that contain them, such as cookie dough and cake mix. Any recipes that call for raw eggs, such as frostings, should be made with a pasteurized egg supplement.

Do not eat uncooked meat, poultry and fish. Cook meat and poultry to these *inside* temperatures to kill bacteria:

- Roast meat at 325 to 350 degrees Fahrenheit and cook until the inside temperatures reaches 170 degrees.
- Hamburgers and ground beef should reach 160 degrees.

- 🔥 Meat-loaf should reach 170 degrees.

- 🔥 Pre-cooked ham should reach 140 degrees, uncooked 165 degrees.

- 🔥 Chicken and turkey should reach 185 degrees, or be cooked until the juices run clear.

- 🔥 Pork should be cooked until inside temperatures reach 185 degrees.

When reheating leftovers, temperatures should reach 165 degrees. Soups and sauces should be boiled for one minute.

Beware of eating raw shellfish. Oysters, clams, and mussels are less likely to be contaminated with bacteria when they are harvested from cold water, thus the saying, only eat shellfish in months that have an "r."

Gena For Dinner

After weeks of preparation I was determined to ask Gena to dinner. We met *coincidentally* in the meat department at the local grocery store. I introduced myself and mentioned we have children in the same baseball league. She smiled, confirming our familiarity, and we made with pleasantries. Then I asked, "Have you ever had sautéed Steak Diane?" (Easy meal, fancy name for steak with sauce on it, and steak sounds so indulgent.) I'll spare the details, but Gena and I had a delicious dinner together and got along quite well. And though she was a little upset when I wouldn't serve her that fourth glass of wine, she *really* enjoyed the chocolate and strawberries.

Let's Eat

Cooking an occasional meal for someone like Gena is easily handled from a cookbook. But the challenge of putting a variety of everyday menus together that children will eat can present a challenge. (Beans and weinies only go so far.) That's why the following menus and recipes are child-friendly, as well as fast and easy. They are separated into seven categories:

Basic breakfast ideas: These breakfast menus do not require a recipe and are easy to cook. Some come from a box, and are simply prepared in a toaster.

Breakfast side dishes: These are designed to complete a balanced breakfast with little effort.

Basic dinner ideas: These dinner menus do not require a recipe and are easy to cook. Many menus and items are found frozen, in cans, boxes, or seasoned bags.

Fast and easy: These dinner menus include recipes and can be prepared in 30 minutes or less.

One pan wonders: Anyone who hates doing dishes will appreciate these dinner recipes for a balanced meal in one pan.

Basic dinner side dishes: These side dishes are designed to complete a meal with little effort and please most children. Combine any of these with the basic dinner or fast and easy menus for a complete meal.

Hassle-free side dishes: These side dishes are prepared in minutes and without cooking in a pan. Combine these with the fast and easy menus for a balanced meal.

Breakfast favorites

(Recipes not included)

Breakfast Main Dish:	Low-Fat Version Use:
Cereal	Skim or low-fat milk (cereal is already low-fat)
Pancakes	Skim or low-fat milk and egg substitute
Waffles	Skim or low-fat milk and egg substitute
Eggs, fried, scrambled, poached, omelette, boiled	Egg substitute and fat-free cooking spray
Breakfast tacos	Fat-free or low-fat ingredients, egg substitute
French toast	Skim or low-fat milk and egg substitute
Egg sandwich, on toast, muffin, croissant, bagel	Fat-free or low-fat ingredients, egg substitute
Oatmeal	Oatmeal is fat-free; eat as much as you like

Breakfast Side Dishes:	Low-Fat Version Use:
Toast, bagels, muffins, spreads	Fat-free or low-fat croissants, biscuits
Fruit	Fruit is fat-free; eat as much as you like
Bacon	Low-fat turkey bacon
Sausage	Fat-free or low-fat varieties
Ham	Fat-free or low-fat varieties
Steak	Small portion size and trim the fat
Potatoes	Small portion sizes and fry in low-fat butter

Corned beef hash	Small portion size and low-fat varieties
Grits	Skim or low-fat milk and butter
Yogurt	Fat-free or low-fat varieties

Basic Dinner Ideas

(Recipes not included)

Dinner-Main Dish:	**Low-Fat Version Use:**
French bread pizza	Low-fat or fat-free cheese and pepperoni
Hot dogs	Low-fat or fat-free dogs
Hamburgers	Lean burger, ground turkey, veggie burgers
Sandwich/subs	Low-fat or fat-free cold-cuts, dressings, and cheese
Chicken patty on roll	Low-fat or fat-free chicken patties
Fish sticks/patties	Low-fat or fat-free varieties
Tacos	Lean burger, ground turkey, low-fat cheese
Sloppy Joe's	Lean burger or ground turkey
Bacon lettuce and tomato	Low-fat or fat-free bacon sandwich
Grilled cheese sandwich	Low-fat or fat-free cheese and butter
Sausage on a hot-dog bun	Low-fat or fat-free varieties

Basic Dinner Side Dishes

(Recipes not included)

Dinner Side dishes:	**Low-Fat Version Use:**
Frozen potatoes varieties (french-fries, tater tots)	Bake in the oven

Mashed potatoes	Low-fat or fat-free butter and milk or use chicken broth
Canned/frozen vegetables	Low-fat or fat-free butter
Chips (any variety)	Low-fat baked, or reduced-fat chips
Crackers(any variety)	Low-fat or fat-free crackers
Rice	Low-fat or fat-free butter
Beans	Low-fat or fat-free varieties
Chili	Low-fat or fat-free varieties
Soup	Low-fat or fat-free varieties
Macaroni and cheese	Low-fat or fat-free milk and butter
Dinner biscuits	Low-fat or fat-free butter
Corn-bread	Low-fat or fat-free butter
Pickles	Fat-free, but watch the sodium

Hassle Free Side Dishes

(Recipes not included)

Hassle Free Side Dishes:	**Low-Fat Version Use:**
Corn on the cob (six minutes for each ear) in a microwave	Low-fat or fat-free butter
Salad	Low-fat or fat-free dressings
Baked potato	Low-fat or fat-free butter and toppings
Deli prepared salads and side dishes	Limit portions; avoid oil or mayonnaise dressings
Coleslaw or cabbage	Low-fat or fat-free dressings
Canned/frozen vegetables, prepared in the microwave	Low-fat or fat-free butter

Fresh fruit	Eat as much as you like
Cottage cheese	Low-fat or fat-free varieties
Fruit cocktail	Reduced calorie or light varieties
Cranberry sauce	Fat-free eat all you want
Any frozen dish that has microwave directions	Low-fat or fat-free varieties

One Pan Meals

(Recipes included)

Barbecue Chicken from the Oven: Place cut chicken in a baking pan. Add one bottle of barbecue sauce, and bake for one hour at 350 degrees. Serve with your choice of hassle-free side dish.

LOW-FAT TIP: *Use skinless chicken.*

Chicken and Rice: Mix two cups of instant rice, one can of concentrated mushroom soup, and one can of milk in an oven-safe pan or casserole dish. Place cut chicken on top of the rice, and bake covered for one hour at 350 degrees. *Optional:* Top with shredded cheese and bake uncovered for five to ten additional minutes or until the cheese is melted. Serve with your choice of hassle-free side dish.

LOW-FAT TIP: *Use skinless chicken or breast, low-fat cheese, and low-fat/low-sodium soup.*

Oven Fried Chicken: Mix one egg and ¼ cup of milk in a serving bowl. In a large storage bag or second serving bowl, mix two cups of bread crumbs with ½ teaspoon of paprika,

½ teaspoon of salt (optional), and ½ teaspoon of pepper. Dip eight pieces of skinless chicken in the egg mixture and coat evenly. Place the chicken in the bread crumbs and pat to coat thoroughly. Position the chicken on a baking dish sprayed with a non-stick coating and refrigerate for 15 minutes. Cook at 400 degrees for one hour. Serve with your choice of hassle free side dish.

NOTE: *The egg and milk coating may be substituted by spreading non-fat yogurt on the chicken before covering with bread crumbs and the bread crumbs may be seasoned to taste. There are also numerous varieties of oven frying coatings from a box. Some even include a baking bag that make clean up a snap.*

LOW-FAT TIP: *Use skinless chicken and egg substitute.*

Pan-Roasted Chicken: Season four to six pieces of boneless chicken breast with paprika and pepper. Brown two minutes per side in an oven-safe skillet with two tablespoons of olive oil and remove. Add three cups of carrots, three cups of potatoes, two teaspoons of oregano, and ½ cup of chicken broth. *Optional:* Onions, turnips or other desired vegetables) Cook for five minutes. Return chicken to the skillet, cover with lid or foil, and bake at 400 degrees for 25 minutes or until vegetables are tender. Add a hassle-free side dish, if desired.

LOW-FAT TIP: *Use skinless chicken breast.*

Beef Stew: In a four-quart saucepan, brown 1½ pounds of cubed beef and drain. Add one small cut onion, three to five cubed potatoes, two chopped carrots, one can of stewed tomatoes, one cup of water, one to two chopped stalk(s) of celery, one beef bouillon cube, one can of whole corn (or mixed vegetables), salt and pepper to taste. Simmer over a medium heat for one hour or until the potatoes are soft.

NOTE: *If you have children that do not like onions, celery, or tomatoes, combine these ingredients with the cup of water in a blender and puree. Children will never know they are eating them.*

LOW-FAT TIP: *Use a cut of meat with little fat, reduce meat portions, and increase the vegetables.*

Pot Roast: In a covered roasting pan, place a one to three pound beef roast with one small chopped onion, three to five cubed potatoes, two chopped carrots, one can of stewed tomatoes, one cup of water, one to two cut stalk(s) of celery, two beef bouillon cubes, one can of whole corn (or mixed vegetables), and salt and pepper to taste. Bake at 350 degrees allowing 30 minutes for each pound of meat or until the potatoes are soft.

LOW-FAT TIP: *Use lean meat, reduce meat por tions, and increase the vegetables.*

Chicken Soup: Place a cut skinless chicken in a six to eight quart saucepan or stock pot. Add one can of condensed chicken broth, chopped celery, onions, and carrots. Cover with water, salt and pepper to taste, and simmer for one hour or until the chicken is tender and pulls away from the bone. Add soup noodles or rice in the last ten to 15 minutes of cooking and serve.

LOW-FAT TIP: *Use skinless chicken and skim off any grease before serving.*

Stir Fry: There are stir-fry packages for beef, chicken, pork, and seafood in your grocer's frozen food section. Most contain everything but the entree seafood or meat needed for an easy to prepare stir fry. The directions are easy: Add a tablespoon of oil to a deep frying pan or wok, stir-fry the entrée seafood or meat, add the frozen ingredients, water, sauce, and simmer. This dish is perfect over rice and with egg rolls purchased from your grocer's deli. Then use a second pan to prepare fried rice, soup, or a simple chow mein as tasty alternatives. (Many delis sell popular side dishes to complement any meal.)

After preparing a frozen variety of stir fry, try building one. Buy each ingredient fresh and customize the selection of vegetables to individual family taste. For example, my children love the extra broccoli and don't miss the peppers, while I prefer extra mushrooms and can't believe bamboo is considered food!

Sauces vary from homemade versions made from simple combinations of soy sauce and water, to more complex recipes that call for graded orange peels. There are also palate-pleasing packages that require only the addition of water, although my favorite comes from a bottle. Selections are wide, allowing one to add as much or as little sauce as desired. Simply add a tablespoon of oil to a deep frying pan or wok, stir-fry the entree, add the fresh ingredients and sauce, and then simmer. (If stir-fry is to be part of a regular menu plan, purchase a stir-fry cookbook and a wok.)

LOW-FAT TIP: *Use skinless seafood or chicken, lean cuts of meat, pour off any grease before adding vegetables, and use reduced sodium/fat sauces.*

Chicken-Mushroom Risotto: In a three to four quart saucepan, brown one pound of cubed, skinless chicken in one tablespoon of margarine or butter. Remove and set aside.

In the same saucepan, add one tablespoon of margarine or butter, one cup uncooked long grain rice, one chopped carrot, one small onion (optional), and cook over medium heat, stirring until rice is brown. Add one can (10 ounces) of low sodium, clear chicken broth, one can (10 ounces) condensed cream of mushroom soup, and ⅛ teaspoon of pepper. Bring to a boil, cover, and simmer for 15 minutes, stirring occasionally.

Add ½ cup of frozen peas or mixed vegetables and the reserved cooked chicken. Cover and cook for five minutes, stirring occasionally. Serve when the rice is tender and the liquid is absorbed.

LOW-FAT TIP: *Use skinless chicken, low-fat margarine, and low-fat or low-sodium soup.*

Cheesy Noodles with Tuna: In a 10-inch deep-dish frying pan, cook three packages of chicken flavored Ramen Noodle Soup and set aside.

In the same skillet, over medium heat, melt margarine or butter; then cook one package (10 ounces) of thawed mixed vegetables and one clove of minced garlic for two minutes, stirring often.

Stir in one can (10 ounces) of condensed cream of mushroom soup and ¾ cup of milk. Add 1½ cups of mozzarella cheese and ⅛ teaspoon of pepper. Cook until the cheese melts, stirring occasionally.

Stir in the boiled noodles and one can of drained tuna broken into chunks. Heat thoroughly (two to five minutes), stirring occasionally.

LOW-FAT TIP: *Use low-fat margarine, soup, milk, and cheese, and tuna packed in water.*

Fast and Easy (30 Minutes or Less)

(Main Dishes-Recipes Included)

In each of the grill recipes, substitute for a grill by placing the meat or fish five inches from an oven broiler.

Chicken from the Grill: Marinate, cut skinless chicken for 30 minutes or more (overnight, if possible) in teriyaki sauce, Italian dressing, or any marinade made for chicken. Season to taste, and grill for 15 to 20 minutes. Basting with barbecue sauce during the last five to ten minutes is optional. Add side dishes and serve.

LOW-FAT TIP: *Use skinless chicken.*

Steak from the Grill: Marinate steak for 30 minutes or more (overnight, if possible) in teriyaki sauce, soy sauce, or any marinade made for steak. Season to taste and grill for 10 to 20 minutes, turning occasionally. Add side dishes and serve.

LOW-FAT TIP: *Use a cut of meat with little fat, reduce meat portion, and increase the vegetables served with it.*

Pork from the Grill: Marinate pork chops or center cut loin for 30 minutes or more (over night, if possible) in teriyaki, or any marinade made for pork. Season to taste and grill for 10 to 20 minutes, turning occasionally. Add side dishes and serve.

Marinade Option: In a dish large enough to hold the pork, combine three teaspoons of soy sauce, three tablespoons of lime juice, three tablespoons of apricot preserves, one table spoon Dijon-style mustard, and one clove (or ½ teaspoon) of minced garlic. Save about ¼ cup for basting and place the pork in the marinade, turning to coat evenly. Cover the dish and place it in the refrigerator for two hours, turning the pork at least once.

LOW-FAT TIP: *Use a cut of meat with little fat, reduce meat portions, and increase the vegetables.*

French Dip: In a small sauce pan, add two cups of water, four beef bouillon cubes and simmer. Heat deli-sliced roast beef (one pound will make four to six sandwiches) in the oven, covered with bouillon broth at 350 degrees for 10 minutes, or microwave to serving temperature. Slice fresh Italian rolls lengthwise, add beef, mozzarella cheese (sliced or grated), and bake for 6 to 12 minutes or till the cheese is melted and the roll is crispy. Serve sandwich with a small bowl of beef bouillon for dipping, and side dish. (French fries are perfect.)

LOW-FAT TIP: *Use a low-fat or fat-free cut of meat.*

The Ultimate Baked Potato: Wash each potato and microwave for four to six minutes. Slice open and season with one of the following taste sensations or create your own master piece.

Pizza flavor: Pizza sauce, mozzarella cheese, pepperoni

Italian flavor: Spaghetti sauce, parmesan cheese

Taco flavor: Salsa, cheese, lettuce, tomato, taco sauce

All American flavor: Butter, sour cream, bacon bits, cheese, chives

Texas flavor: Chili, cheese

For that more conventional taste, wrap in tin foil and bake at 400 degrees for 45 minutes.

LOW-FAT TIP: *Use low-fat or fat-free toppings.*

Pasta: Spaghetti and other varieties of pasta with red sauce can be fast, easy, or comfortably slow.

Fast: There are store-brand sauces that are very good, or close enough that they can be doctored to taste with a little extra sauce, salt, pepper, basil, sugar, or seasoned stewed tomatoes. My family prefers meat, so I add one pound of cooked ground beef, seasoned to taste. Simply mix the meat with the sauce, simmer for 10 minutes and serve over pasta. (Don't have time to cook burger? Add a can of baby clams and course black pepper for a spicy clam sauce.)

Easy: In a six to eight quart saucepan, add one 14-ounce can of Italian recipe stewed tomatoes, four 14-ounce cans of tomato sauce, two tablespoons basil, and (optional) one teaspoon of sugar. This sauce is savory, with or without meat, in just 10 to 30 minutes.

Comfortably Slow: Before creating the premium recipe, we must discuss meatballs, recipe size, and cooking times. First, this recipe calls for meatballs, not ground burger. Meatballs add flavor to the sauce as they cook. (They also provide great sandwiches and subs when topped with mozzarella . . . mmm.)

Meatballs: Mix one to three pounds of ground beef with one to two eggs, two to four wet pieces of bread, approximately ¼ cup of onion chopped fine (my son calls them onion specks), season to taste with salt and pepper, and mix thoroughly. In a frying pan, cook golf-ball size meatballs until brown, turning occasionally, careful not to over-cook, then add to the sauce. (This recipe also makes tasty hamburgers and meatloaf.)

Next is portion size. Although this recipe makes six to eight quarts, don't hesitate to double or triple the recipe. I personally make 16 to 18 quarts of sauce and 10 pounds of meatballs. I freeze some and prepare everything from lasagna to ravioli simply by heating the sauce.

Then there is cooking time. The secret to thick, hearty sauce is the same as the key to great sex, *cook it as long as you can!* My best calls for a two-hour simmer, stirring occasionally, a good bottle of wine, and Gena.

The Ultimate Red sauce: In a six to eight quart saucepan add one 14-ounce can of Italian recipe stewed tomatoes, four 15-ounce cans of tomato sauce, one teaspoon sugar, one tablespoon basil, one small can of mushrooms, one or two cloves of garlic (or one teaspoon of minced), and ⅓ diced onion (approximately ¼ cup). (Should your children dislike chunky sauce, puree the stewed tomatoes, mushrooms, onion, and garlic.)

Optional: Add two ounces (½ can) of tomato paste. Place the sauce on low heat as the meatballs are cooking.

Optional Ingredient: Pork. That's right, pork. Brown one to two pounds of pork ribs or neck bones in the same pan that was used for the meatballs and add them to the sauce. Allow the sauce to simmer without burning until the meat falls from the bone.

For pasta, consider serving shells or large easy-to-eat noodles for kids. My children still don't have the hang of twirling spaghetti, and I hate the extra work it causes at laundry time. There are also many great varieties of pasta in the frozen/refrigerated section at your local grocery store.

LOW-FAT TIP: *Use a lean cut of ground beef and a small portion of pork.*

Ham from the Grill or Oven: Buy a large three to seven pound cooked ham and have the butcher slice ½-inch steaks. (At this price, it is a good idea to have a pound or two sliced for sandwiches.) Grill four to eight minutes, add side dishes, and serve. Marinade Option: In a dish large enough to hold the ham slices, combine six teaspoons soy sauce, three table spoons lime juice, three tablespoons apricot preserves, one tablespoon Dijon-style mustard and one clove (or ½ teaspoon) of minced garlic. Save about ¼ cup for basting and place the ham in the marinade turning to coat evenly. Cover the dish and place it in the refrigerator for two hours, turning the ham at least once.

LOW-FAT TIP: *Use a low-fat ham.*

Fish from the Grill: Marinate fish fillets or steaks for 30 minutes or more in Italian dressing or any marinade made for fish. Brush oil on the grill before it gets hot and cook fish 10 minutes per inch of thickness, or till the center is no longer translucent, basting at least once while cooking. (Shrimp, scallops, and lobster are just as easy.) Add side dishes and serve.

LOW-FAT TIP: *Use no-fat dressing and eat as much as you like.*

Pizza: It is a weekly tradition at my house. I make several variations of dough in my bread machine and make my own sauce. But one doesn't need to make sauce and dough from scratch to make great pizza. Pizza dough/crusts can be purchased in numerous varieties. There are prepared crusts ready to bake, packages of dough ready to use, packages that simply require the addition of water, and some bakeries that sell bread dough by the pound (1½ pounds for a large pizza works well). Pizza sauce can be made from scratch or purchased in a can or jar.

Whichever is used, simply grease a pizza pan, knead the dough to shape, spread the sauce, add mozzarella cheese, pepperoni and other toppings, if desired. Then, place the pizza in an oven heated to 400 degrees for about 10 to 20 minutes. For a crispy crust, place the pizza directly on the oven rack for the last one to two minutes of cooking.

No time to knead dough? Try french bread or hamburger buns.

LOW-FAT TIP: *Use low-fat or fat-free toppings.*

Turkey from the Grill: Marinate turkey breast for 30 minutes or more (overnight, if possible) in teriyaki sauce or any marinade made for chicken. Season to taste and grill for 15 to 20 minutes. Add side dishes and serve.

LOW-FAT TIP: *Eat as much as you like.*

Rate Your Cooking

If these questions were asked at your next meal, what best describes the responses that would be given? Circle your answer and total your scores for an assessment of your cooking skills.

1) Should I serve it?
   1 Proudly.
   2 With reservation.
   3 To whom?

2) Should I save it?
   1 Can't, it is all gone.
   2 There is nothing to save it in.
   3 When is trash day?

3) Will the dogs eat it (without getting sick)?
   1 Yes.
   2 No.
   3 No, they had this last night.

4) Should we eat it again?
   1 Yes, but not for breakfast.
   2 Not before it is refrigerated for two weeks.
   3 Depends; what was it?

5) Who wants seconds?
     1 I do! I do!
     2 Not me. I'm stuffed, got dessert?
     3 Qué?

Total points:

     5 to 8:   No need to question your culinary skills. Bon
                appetite.
     9 to 12:   Yes you can prepare food, but can you live on
                it?
     13 to 15: Stick with frozen food, and remember, *remove
                the wrapper before heating.*

Finally, if you have a picky eater, avoid punishing them for
not eating. As long as your child is growing normally and gaining weight there is probably little to worry about. Try to provide three balanced meals a day, even though most children will
only eat two full meals a day. Also, limit snacking to two nutri-
tious snacks each day. If your child won't eat the family dinner,
don't prepare another meal for them. He/she won't starve miss-
ing a meal or two here or there, and preparing a second meal
will only create other problems.

Children's Safety

Home Safety

The Dallas Morning News, January 15, 1996: "A 3-year-old east Dallas boy whose brother set fire to curtains while playing with matches late Saturday became the fifth Dallas child this year to die in a house fire, Dallas fire officials said."

The Fort Worth Star Telegram, June 23, 1998: "A 1-year-old girl who was left unattended in a bathtub for a few moments drowned yesterday at her south Grand Prairie home, police said."

Every day, children are injured or killed in their own homes by accidents such as these. Baby hazards are everywhere. Carolyn Poirot, in *The Fort Worth Star Telegram* of September 8, 1998, cited National Safety Council statistics stating that each year 8,000 children under the age of 15 die of accidental injuries and 50,000 more are permanently disabled in accidents in and around the home.

Often there are undetected dangers and children, with their natural curiosities, will find them. The following precautions can help make your home safe.

- Never leave small children (under age seven) unattended.

- Never carry hot drinks and children at the same time.

- Guns and children don't mix.

- Use gates at both the tops and bottoms of stairways.

- Use unbreakable glassware and dishes, and never use glass in the bathroom.

- Use safety latches on low cupboards and drawers.

- Keep doors to dangerous rooms (bathrooms, basements, and so on) closed at all times.

- Keep appliance cords out of reach.

- Keep electrical appliances out of children's bathrooms.

- Keep heavy objects out of reach.

- Keep matches and lighters out of reach.

- ◎ Keep a child's crib safe from dangerous toys, pillows, and bedding.

- ◎ Keep your fireplace safe, clean, and covered.

- ◎ Keep your yard safe by keeping toys picked up, pools gated, fences latched, lawn tools stored, and anything else presenting danger removed.

- ◎ Do not overload electrical outlets and cover unused outlets.

- ◎ When cooking, keep pan handles to the back of the stove.

- ◎ Lower the water temperature in the hot water heater to 120 degrees.

- ◎ Avoid furniture with sharp corners, edges, or glass.

- ◎ Lock or keep all medicines out of reach.

- ◎ Regulate, inspect, and maintain safe toys.

- ◎ Do not use a waterbed for children as there's a risk of suffocation or drowning.

- ◎ Keep your automobile locked and always use car seats and/or safety belts.

Before declaring your home safe, visit the garage, where there are usually enough chemicals to build a small bomb. Always keep weed killer, bug spray, gas, antifreeze, other poisonous chemicals, and dangerous tools locked and out of reach.

Other child safety information can be found on the Internet at Safe Within, www.safewithin.com.

Home Emergencies

Peter recalled an accident his daughter had while visiting him. "I was teaching her how to ride a bike. She wasn't wearing a helmet when she fell and hit her head. She was unconscious and bleeding from the ears. All I could think of was, I wish I knew what to do!" Here are some ways to be prepared for an emergency.

+ Learn CPR.

+ Keep all emergency numbers posted and current. This should include: fire, police, hospital, family doctor(s), dentist, pharmacist, schools, child care providers, poison control center, work numbers, the child's mother, and an emergency contact.

+ Keep a well-stocked first aid kit and first aid manual.

+ Install fire extinguishers and instruct children on their proper use.

+ Install and inspect smoke alarms.

+ Consider an in-home security system with a panic button.

+ Keep current school pictures and videos of your children.

Poisoning

In that same *Star Telegram* article, Carolyn Poirot tells a story of a mother who stepped out of the laundry room to answer the phone. The next thing she knew, her baby had pulled a bottle of bleach with a loose lid from a low shelf, and was sitting in a puddle of the caustic chemical. The baby's bottom was severely burned by the time her mother could get the child's bleach-soaked diaper off.

The Texas Poison Center Network provides the following advice on Emergency Action for Poisoning.

Inhaled Poison:

Immediately get the person to fresh air. Avoid breathing fumes. Open doors and windows wide. If victim is not breathing, start artificial respiration.

Poison on the Skin:

Remove contaminated clothing and flood skin with water for 10 minutes. Then wash gently with soap and water and rinse.

Poison in the Eye:

Flood the eye with lukewarm (not hot) water poured from a large glass two or three inches from the eye. Repeat for 15 minutes. Have patient blink as much as possible while flooding the eye. Do not force the eyelid open.

Swallowed Poison:

Unless patient is unconscious, having convulsions, or cannot swallow, give a glass (two to eight ounces) of water immediately, then call for professional advice about whether you should make the patient vomit.

Every home should keep syrup of ipecac on hand; it is used to induce vomiting for non-corrosive poisons. However, do not induce vomiting unless instructed by a doctor or the Poison Control Center. If a child ingests a solid poison such as pills or mothballs, wipe away any toxic remnants from his or her mouth with a wet washcloth. Then call the local Poison Control Center or 9-1-1 and be prepared to answer the following questions:

- ☠ What did your child ingest?
- ☠ What are his/her symptoms?
- ☠ How old is your child and what is his/her weight?
- ☠ How long has it been since the poison was ingested?
- ☠ Does your child have any other health problems?
- ☠ Is he/she taking any other medications?

Stranger Danger

The Dallas Morning News, January 14, 1996: "A 9-year-old girl was abducted Saturday afternoon while riding her bicycle in an east central Arlington neighborhood, police said. Police say Amber Hagerman, a student at Arlington's Berry Elementary, yelled and fought with the man who pulled her from her bicycle about 3:15 p.m. from a parking lot at Abram Street and Brown Drive. A witness told police he saw the man force Amber into a full-sized black pickup truck. Amber was found dead four days later in a creek bed with her throat slashed."

The days of carefree living are over. A day doesn't pass without a report on child abduction, molestation, or murder. These senseless attacks target children of all ages and are the nightmare of every parent. It's crucial that both fathers and their children understand the dangers from strangers and what actions can avoid fatal situations. Enforce and educate your children on the following rules.

✘ Never accept anything from a stranger.

✘ Say "no" to anyone that makes you feel nervous or uncomfortable.

✘ Never talk to strangers! This includes people who stop on the street asking for directions or help finding a pet. Say, "I'll get my dad."

✘ Run away if a stranger offers you a ride, candy, or a gift of any kind.

✘ Scream for help or run away to a safe place (store, home) if somebody grabs or demands that you go with them.

✘ Never believe a stranger if they say, "Your dad says you should come with me."

✘ Never tell anyone aloud you are alone.

✗   Always keep your house key out of sight.

Nearby Dangers

The Dallas Morning News, March 24, 1998: "A church pastor convicted of sexually assaulting two teenage sisters in his congregation should spend the rest of his life in prison, a judge decided Monday."

Some reports estimate there are 500,000 cases of sexual assault on children each year. Surprisingly enough, these molestations are more likely to be from a family member, relative, step-parent, girlfriend, coach, or teacher, than a stranger. This means a father should suspect everyone and end any unhealthy relationship children may be in. Watch for any of these warning signs:

✔   Any adult that singles out your child with special attention.

✔   Unusual activity from a care giver, especially if they were found through an ad.

✔   Strange behavior from anyone in contact with your child.

✔   Unexpected changes in the actions of your children.

✔   Someone suddenly entering your family circle.

✔   Anyone asking inappropriate questions of your child.

✔   Anyone who touches your child excessively or inappropriately.

✔   Any adult who spends excessive time with your child.

✔   Anyone who plans trips especially for your child.

✔   Anyone who provides gifts especially for your child.

✔   Strange behavior from your children when in the presence of a particular adult.

Unsupervised Care

Arlington Metro, "Two toddlers left in the care of their two older brothers died yesterday in a house fire that may have been ignited by a space heater, fire officials said."

Over the years, I have seen my care needs change from an in-home nanny, to after-school programs, and finally to the need for no child care at all. Incredible as it may sound, the most stressful of all for me was leaving my children alone. When the time finally came that I no longer had to pay for day-care, my first thought was, "That extra money will sure come in handy."

Beware, nothing is without cost. Children who are unsupervised are more likely to use drugs or alcohol, smoke, or have lower grades, than those who are supervised. Fathers need to pay close attention when a child is left alone, and to stay involved. If a child comes home with green hair, it is a sign that dad is not in touch. If Dad says, "There is nothing I can do about it," he is out of control, too. When are children mature enough to be on their own? Most authorities suggest not to leave a child under the age of 10 or 11 alone for more than two to three hours at a time, unless he or she is with an older sibling. And before leaving children alone prepare your house and children for the following situations:

Never leave a child alone without preparation. A father should start preparing children for time alone a little at a time by taking short trips away during the day. Start with trips to the store, bank, or other brief errands.

Never leave unsupervised children in a home with guns. Everyday in this country 10 children are killed by handguns.

Keep a spare key outside at a neighbors house for emergencies. Children will inevitably forget or lose their key and they will need a spare. However, do not leave a key in an obvious place such as under a doormat or in one of those stupid rocks.

Set house rules. This should include a policy for visitors, cooking, telephone use, television, and neighborhood boundaries. Children must have a clear definition of expected behavior when they are left alone.

Set limits on dangerous toys, bikes, skateboards, or pools. If a child hits his or her head or has an accident in a pool when there is no one around, it could cost a life.

Set limits on places of negative influence and boundaries for outside travel. Do not allow children to hang out in places or with people that might lead to trouble.

Set behavior limits with siblings. Teach children that they are not to hit each other.

Teach how to answer the door when children are alone. Instruct children not to open the door or to let a stranger know that they are alone. Have them say, "My dad can't come to the door right now," or simply instruct them not to answer the door at all.

Keep windows and doors locked at all times.

Teach proper phone use. Instruct children to never tell a caller, "My dad isn't here." Rather, have them say, "My dad can't come to the phone. Can I take a message?" Children must also be able to ask for and take a message. I hated coming home to, "Dad, some girl called!" After taking a message, a child should be instructed to call or page dad.

Teach children all important personal information. Children should not be left alone unless they know their full name, phone number, address, and other important numbers such as dad's work and pager number. This should be taught starting at the age of three.

Tell a trusted neighbor or relative when children will be left alone.

Another hidden cost when children are left alone is that things get broken, dad's things! Occasional mishaps are unfortunate, but this is the cost of leaving children alone. So, when this happens, don't punish the children excessively. After all, they're just kids.

A Father's Health

I am a few years away from middle age now and the reflection in the mirror isn't what it used to be. My size 32 waist isn't size 32 anymore, there is gray in my receding hair, and other hair is starting to grow from the strangest places. Thank heavens my plumbing still works.

My 20-year-old son reflects the image I still remember. I wonder if I had made healthier decisions at his age would I be starting the fourth quarter of my life ahead by a touchdown instead of losing by 35 points?

The offensive strategy on page one of the game plan of life is exercise. Exercise is important for strengthening and building the immune system, gaining energy, losing weight and fighting off illnesses such as cancer (including prostate), heart disease, and high blood pressure. Exercise also reduces stress and depression, while suppressing the appetite, helping one sleep better, and heightening sexual desire. Exercise is the foundation of youth, but who has time?

I met Ron, a custodial father of two, who exercises on a regular basis, about a year ago. I asked him, "How do you manage to find the time to exercise without feeling guilty?"

He said, "I'll never forget the time I was on an airplane with my children and the flight attendant went through the routine, 'In case of a sudden change in cabin pressure, an oxygen mask will drop from the overhead compartment.' She also told the adults to place the mask over their face before assisting their children with theirs. I thought I should help my children first. It would be selfish to save myself before my daughters. Then it dawned on me. If I couldn't breathe, I would be unable to help my children. This is the way I look at exercising, I would feel guilty if I didn't."

"Besides, a basic exercise program is simple," Ron added. "With just 30 minutes of sustained, aerobic exercise (running, walking, cycling, swimming) three to five days a week, one can dramatically improve health, energy, and the quality of life. That's not a lot of time to invest in staying healthy. And if you can't put a program together yourself, go buy a men's magazine. The are many different ways to start and maintain an exercise program."

For most bachelor parents, finding time between a job, commuting, kids' homework, and domestic chores, 30 minutes can be a difficult thing to find, especially if exercising includes a 30 to 40 minute drive to a gym. "When my children were small, and I was unable to afford a sitter, I would work out around my house," said Ron. "I pushed the coffee table to the side, watched aerobic videos and did squats, crunches, and push-ups. When I wanted to include strength training, I bought a set of weights at a garage sale for ten bucks and started lifting on my patio. Even house chores like cutting the grass became part of my workout. Now, I try to include my children whenever I can. We in-line skate, ride bikes, and play tennis together. This is great for my parenting time, and we have a lot of fun staying healthy. Not to mention the women one can meet while working out."

Page two of our game plan is a sensible diet. The following dietary guidelines have been developed by the Department of Health and Human Services and the U.S. Department of Agriculture, and represent the best, most current advice for healthy Americans two years and older. They reflect recommendations of health and nutrition experts who agree that enough is known about the effect of diet on health to encourage certain eating practices. The seven guidelines are:

Eat a variety of foods to get the energy (calories), protein, vitamins, minerals, and fiber you need for good health.

Maintain a healthy weight to reduce your chances of having high blood pressure, heart disease, stroke, certain cancers, and the most common kinds of diabetes.

Choose a diet low in fat, saturated fat, and cholesterol to reduce your risk of heart disease and certain types of cancer. Because fat contains more than twice the calories of an equal amount of carbohydrates or protein, a diet low in fat can help you maintain a healthy weight.

Choose a diet with plenty of vegetables, fruits, and grain products that provide needed vitamins, minerals, fiber, and complex carbohydrates. They also are generally lower in fat.

Use sugars only in moderation. A diet with lots of sugars has too many calories, too few nutrients, and can contribute to tooth decay.

Use salt and other forms of sodium only in moderation to help reduce your risk of high blood pressure.

If you drink alcoholic beverages, do so in moderation. Alcoholic beverages supply calories, but little or no nutrients. Drinking alcohol is also the cause of many health problems, accidents, and can lead to addiction.

Page three of our game plan is a defense against aging by using the following formations:

Quit smoking (or better yet, don't start). In addition to causing lung-cancer, heart disease, bad breath, and skin damage, smoking reduces blood flow to the penis and may cause erectile dysfunction (ED) and impotence.

Exercise. Studies show that men who exercise have half the risk of colon cancer than those who don't. Studies also show that one in three Americans will develop some type of cancer, while athletes average only one in seven.

Have sex on a regular basis. Use it or lose it is the advice here. Regular ejaculations are a good way to keep the prostate healthy and prevent cancer. Sex is also a great way to reduce stress and increase the desire for life.

Drink in moderation. While there is evidence that moderate drinking (especially red wine), may be good for the heart and lowers the risk for cancer (like prostate), excessive alcohol (more than two drinks a day), can increase the risk of cancer and cirrhosis of the liver. In addition, alcoholics are more likely to suffer from erectile dysfunction.

Laugh a little. Laughter will raise the heart beat, increase breathing, and can reduce the aging caused by stress.

Get plenty of sleep. Experts call a good night's sleep a therapeutic daily elixir, essential to a physical energy, a clear mind, and long healthy life.

Find spirituality. A healthy spirit can give a sense of direction, fulfillment, and well-being. There are also opinions that spirituality contributes to better health and a longer life.

Cut the fat from food like whole milk and cheese, processed food, and red meat. This is the stuff that clogs arteries and increases the risk of cancer and heart disease.

Drink plenty of water. The average man should drink about eight glasses a day to provide essential fluids and minerals.

Maintain a sensible weight. Overweight people are more likely to develop heart at tacks, strokes, and diabetes.

Don't diet. Losing weight by not eating is temporary. In most cases when dieting stops, the lost weight returns along with a little extra. Maintaining weight comes from exercising and eating right, every day.

Eat breakfast (especially if weight loss is on the agenda). A car won't go far without gas in the tank. The same is true with our bodies.

Check your tools. According American Cancer Society's *Cancer Facts and Figures-1999* (reprinted with permission), have your prostate checked, including a Prostate-Specific Antigen test (PSA), every year after age 50 or age 40 if there is a family history of cancer or you are African-American. And according to the Testicular Cancer Resource Center, men should check their testicles monthly. The purpose of the self-exam is to become familiar with one's testicles. This way, if anything changes, you will know and be aware that cancer is a possibility.

The self-exam is best performed after a warm shower or bath by standing in front of a mirror and checking for swelling on the scrotum skin. Then examine each testicle by gently rolling them between the thumb and fingers, checking for lumps. A normal testicle feels smooth, egg shaped, and firm. Feel around for any small pea-sized lumps. Any lump, unusual tenderness, enlargement of the scrotum, pain, or feeling of heaviness should be reported to your doctor. Should one testicle be larger than the other, relax, that is normal.

Avoid sun exposure. Too much sun can cause skin cancer, wrinkles, rough skin, light and dark patches, and weaken the immune system.

Read everyday. Try the newspaper or a thought provocative book. Knowledge is power and the key to being able to carry an intelligent conversation.

Finally, our game plan focuses on special teams, vitamins and supplements. According to the Council for Responsible Nutrition, Washington, D.C., there are more than 40 different vitamins and minerals essential for good health that our bodies cannot manufacture. Many of these nutrients play an important role in reducing the risk of common and chronic diseases and illnesses.

The Health Benefits Of Vitamins And Minerals

VITAMIN/MINERAL	HEALTH BENEFIT
Vitamin A	Promotes growth, repair of body tissues, bone formation, and healthy skin and hair. Essential for night vision.
Beta Carotene	Serves as an antioxidant and may help protect against certain cancers, cataracts, and heart disease. Converted to Vitamin A in the body.
Vitamin C	Promotes healthy cell development, wound healing, and resistance to infections. Serves as an antioxidant and may help protect against certain cancers, cataracts, and heart disease.
Vitamin D	Aids in the absorption of calcium and helps build bone mass and prevent bone loss. Helps maintain blood levels of calcium and phosphorous.

Vitamin E   Helps protect cells from free radical injury and is key for normal growth and development. Serves as an antioxidant and may help protect against certain cancers, cataracts, and heart disease.

Vitamin K   Needed for normal blood clotting

Thiamin   Essential for converting carbohydrates to energy. Needed for normal functioning of the nervous system and muscles, including the heart muscle.

Riboflavin   Helps in red blood cell formation, nervous system functioning, and the release of energy from foods. May improve vision and help protect against cataracts.

Niacin   Promotes release of energy from foods and proper nervous system functioning.

Vitamin B-6   Important for metabolizing protein and proper nervous system functioning.

Vitamin B-12   Vital for blood formation and healthy nervous system.

Biotin   Assists in metabolizing fatty acids and utilization of B-vitamins

Folic Acid   Needed for normal growth and development and red blood cell formation.

Pantothenic Acid Aids in normal growth and development.

Calcium   Essential for developing and maintaining healthy bones and teeth. Assists in blood clotting, muscle contraction, and nerve transmission. Helps reduce the risk of osteoporosis.

Chromium	Aids in normal growth and development.
Iron	Necessary for red blood cell formation and function.
Magnesium	Activates nearly 100 enzymes and helps nerve and muscle function.
Phosphorus	Works with calcium to develop and maintain strong bones and teeth. Enhances use of other nutrients.
Potassium	Regulates heartbeat, maintains fluid balance, and helps muscles contract.
Selenium	Essential component of a key antioxidant enzyme. Necessary for normal growth and development.
Zinc	Essential part of more than 100 enzymes involved in digestion, metabolism, reproduction, and wound healing.

It is possible to achieve adequate levels of nutrients through diet, but the fact is that most people don't. A government survey of 21,000 people showed that not a single person surveyed obtained 100 percent of the RDA (Recommended Dietary Allowance) for each nutrient. The National Cancer Institute recommends that people eat at least five servings of fruits and vegetables a day, but unfortunately less than 10 percent of us actually do. In addition, a diet analysis revealed that most

Americans consume inadequate levels of vitamins A, C, E, Thiamin, Riboflavin, B-6, B-12, and Folic Acid as well as Calcium, Iron, Magnesium, Chromium, Selenium, and Zinc. A daily supplement containing these nutrients can help fill the gap between what we actually eat and the amount of nutrients needed to promote optimal health.

Selecting a multi-vitamin/mineral supplement starts by reading the label and looking at the U.S. Recommended Daily Allowance. However, it is important to remember that 100 percent of some minerals would produce a pill too large to swallow. One must look for a supplement that contains the nutrients commonly lacking from a man's diet. One such multiple vitamin and mineral supplement is Mega Men by GNC. It contains a variety of minerals including, Vitamin A, Folic Acid, Zinc, Copper, Magnesium, and Chromium. Mega Men also includes antioxidants, vitamins C and E, and beta-carotene which naturalizes or reverses the damage caused by free radicals. Free radicals are damaged oxygen molecules in the blood stream that are believed to cause aging, wrinkles, liver spots, stiff joints, cancer, clogged arteries, and heart disease. Free radicals are caused by excessive exposure to pollution, sunlight, smoke, alcohol and unsaturated fat.

Mega Men also contains Saw Palmento for prostrate health and Ginseng to increase energy, reduce stress, and enhance intellectual and physical performance.

This is the game plan to a healthy life. We all need a solid performances from offense, defense, and special teams to win.

"Put me in coach. I'm ready!"

Money Matters

The night was silent, the air cool. Around 2 A.M., Stan, woke in a cold sweat. "I'm dreaming. No, I'm having a nightmare," he said. Half asleep, Stan turned on the light. Half-covering his eyes with his hand, he peeked around. When he realized he wasn't dreaming, Stan buried his head in his pillow and screamed.

Stan's nightmare began when he divorced. He was awarded custody of attorney's fees, credit cards debts, and a car payment. In addition he was ordered to pay 25% of his income for child support. The courts gave him everything but his kids. Stan is a self-employed contractor and his lack of disposable income made him struggle to make ends meet. He was soon living paycheck to paycheck, bills were going unpaid, creditors were calling at work, and he was borrowing from one credit card to pay another. Like millions of other newly divorced fathers, Stan owed more then he made. "I knew things were bad when I started using a credit card to buy groceries. I was paying 22% interest on food!"

Needing help, Stan called the Consumer Credit Counseling Service (800-388-CCCS). This nonprofit organization is partially funded by creditors, and offers free or low-cost counseling and education to help develop understandable budgets, and set goals for climbing out of debt. CCCS was able to stop Stan's creditors from harassing him; to freeze finance charges, late fees, and over-limit charges; to lower interest rates; to stop a repossession; and to develop a budget to pay off his debts.

Money Matters: A Money Management Guide For Today's Consumer prepared by CCCS, teaches that if you answer "yes" to any of these questions, you could benefit from their services:

- Are you borrowing money on your credit cards to pay current bills?

- Are you charging everyday expenses on small items?

- Are you paying more than 20 percent of your take-home income for installment purchases and credit card charges?

- 💰 Are you forced to reduce your debt payments to pay for food and housing expenses?

- 💰 Are any of this month's bills coming in before you have paid last month's?

- 💰 Are you unable to save money for anticipated annual and occasional expenses (*e.g.,* insurance premiums, auto repairs, and the like)?

- 💰 Are you borrowing more money before the old loan is paid off?

- 💰 You should know what your total credit indebtedness is. Is it more than you can pay off in 12 months?

- 💰 Do your charge account balances grow each month?

Stan's personal and confidential counselor was Ms. Betty J. Banks, CCCC, CFCE, Senior Vice-President of Education, CCCS Dallas. Ms. Banks was quick to point out the path to economic redemption: "The first thing you must do is take inventory and determine your *have-to's, need-to's,* and *want-to's.*" Ms. Banks stressed including all expenses, not just the obvious ones. "It's very easy to overlook expenses such as alcohol, tobacco products, health club memberships, tolls, and parking, often resulting in an unrealistic budget." Another advantage of listing expenses is being able to see where to save.

Stan said, "When I looked where **all** my money was going, and I mean every cent, it was obvious where I could cut back."

Ms. Banks then asked Stan to write down his short-term goals, such as gift giving, and creating an emergency fund. Then she had him to list his long term goals, such as buying a new home and saving for his retirement. "I've never been asked to do something like this," Stan said. "I didn't think I could see past my debts."

Ms. Banks noted that until goals are written down, there is no commitment and no motivation. Stan said, "Hell, all I have to do is think about bankruptcy and losing what little I have. That provides all the leverage I need." Ms. Banks warned that not everyone is inspired by failure. Some have better luck focusing on the positive aspects of being debt-free and financially secure, while written goals can help provide extra focus.

Another method Ms. Banks recommended was to relate every expense to time. Just figure how many work-hours earn enough to afford a movie, or a trip to a fast food restaurant. Then ask, "Is the expenditure worth it?" Stan has to work more than four hours to earn enough for a dinner date. (However, he determines the worth after the date.)

Ms. Banks then instructed Stan to stop charging and to control his spending. "Don't buy on impulse, stop borrowing, and pay cash for everything possible." She explained that it can take more than 30 years to pay off a $2,500 credit card balance, and you pay up to $6,000 interest if you pay only monthly minimums. Max out one or two cards at this rate, and you will always be in debt. The way Stan figured, he had a 15-year mortgage on his stereo.

Stan's most helpful lesson came when he found out what he should be spending. "Once I had an idea what normal spending was, I had no problem coming up with my own budget." Ms. Banks cautioned that a prescribed budget to fit everyone is impossible. Someone living in California could pay four times the amount for housing as someone living in Texas, and someone paying 30% of his net income for child support will be lower than average in almost every area. Not to mention, people have different values and goals. According to CCCS statistics, a typical budget looks something like this:

Housing	25–28%
Utilities	7–10%
Transportation	5–7%
Food	11–13%
Savings/Medical	5–10%
Debt	18%
Day-care/Child support	16%
Miscellaneous/Clothes	4%

A look at Stan's budget shows housing is high for a single father, and there is no allowance for savings.

Housing/Utilities	30%
Transportation (Insurance/Gas)	15%
Food and clothing	10%
Child support	20%
Debt reduction	15%
Entertainment	5%
Health Care/Miscellaneous	5%

Stan explains, "I spend most of my time at home. My children visit on a regular basis, and I prefer not to have a roommate. So having my own apartment is more important then being a "Disneyland Dad" and blowing $100 every other weekend. That's why I elected to cut back on entertainment and combine food and clothing to make room for child support. I would also like to start building a three month emergency fund, but putting money in the bank to earn two to four percent while paying over 20% on credit cards doesn't make sense. When I have my debts paid, I'll adjust my budget and save."

Some fathers must make major adjustments to meet financial commitments and goals. Raymond, a middle income lab technician, was in a similar situation and shared his experiences: "A budget is not an easy thing to live with. At first, I had to make substantial sacrifices. I needed a roommate, and I was forced to trade my car for a lesser one just to survive." The good news was that Raymond did just fine. Sure, it was tough at first, but in just five years, he was debt free and is now enrolled in CCCS's *Housing Counseling Service*, ready to purchase his own home.

Michael, a custodial father, works on an auto assembly line and has a different set of circumstances. His budget looks like the one below. Notice he pays more than average for housing and has a lower than normal savings budget. "My children have lived in our house since they were born. The last thing I wanted to do after my divorce was disrupt their lives and move. As for savings, I have to save something or I'm in real trouble if my home needs a repair. I'm also fortunate to work at the plant. They provide company uniforms, and I have a good medical plan."

Housing/Utilities	36%
Transportation (Insurance/Gas)	13%
Food	15%
Clothing	3%
Health Care	5%
Entertainment	6%
Savings	3%
Debt reduction	15%
Miscellaneous	4%

Jason, a divorced father of two, is a commercial loan officer and never seems to have enough money to afford entertainment. So, he came up with this remedy: "If you need more cash, go make it. Grab a lawn mower and cut grass, repair cars, start a cleaning service, fix appliances, or type documents. Everyone can do something. The secret to living on a budget is having more money." Here are some other ideas to increase incoming revenue:

 Take on a second job. Consider positions as waiter, bartender, hotel service worker, and catering. (Start by looking in the classified section of the paper.)

 Work overtime.

- Work as a consulting agent.

- Ask for a raise.

- Look for a higher paying position/job.

- Eliminate or reduce optional payroll deductions and lower withholding taxes if you receive a large tax refund.

- Encourage older children to work for their own expenses.

- Buy and sell items such as antiques, autos, stereos, tools, bikes, exercise equipment, or anything that is of interest.

- Make a hobby a business.

- Tutor someone.

- Have a garage sale.

- Stop smoking (or other bad habits).

- Don't gamble.

Not all fathers can find the time or are able to take on a second job. Richard, also a custodial father, said, "My kids aren't old enough to be left alone, and I refuse to pay someone three dollars an hour so I can make six and give 30% back in taxes. If I need more money to go out, I have to spend less." Richard is not alone, and all fathers can benefit from the ways to save money at the end of this chapter.

When each of my single friends were asked for their advice on budgeting, they replied, "The only thing worse than struggling with a budget is not having a budget at all." To take some of the pain out of budgeting and come up with a little extra cash at the end of the month, here are some tips for every major budgeting area:

Auto/Transportation

- 🏍 Car pool.
- 🏍 Ride mass transit whenever possible.
- 🏍 Schedule errands together to reduce the number of trips.
- 🏍 Wash your own car.
- 🏍 Perform simple maintenance (oil changes, tune-ups) at home.
- 🏍 Barter for repairs.
- 🏍 Ask for a discount on all repairs.
- 🏍 Question all repairs and ask for the old part(s).
- 🏍 Pump self-serve gas.
- 🏍 Shop for lower insurance rates every three to four years.
- 🏍 Consolidate your car and home insurance for lower rates.
- 🏍 Increase deductibles in order to lower premiums.
- 🏍 Take defensive driving in order to lower premiums.
- 🏍 Choose a low maintenance car.
- 🏍 Raise your deductible.
- 🏍 Don't insure a sports car.

🏍 Drive a car without payments.

🏍 Drive a car under warranty.

🏍 Buy last year's model.

Banking

💲 Pay yourself first. If you save $25 a week in stocks that gain 10% a year, you will have $104,071 in 22 years.

💲 Avoid ATMs that charge a service fee.

💲 Shop and compare bank fees for overdraft charges, stop payment fees, credit cards, and monthly service charges.

💲 Hold onto your money. Deposit checks immediately and pay bills at the last moment.

💲 Invest and contribute to your company pension plan, 401K, or similar savings program.

💲 Buy checks from a mail order firm. This can save up to 50%. Here are three:

Designer Checks, Inc, PO Box 9222, Anniston, AL 36202

Current Inc., P.O. Box 1900, Colorado Springs, Co 80935

Checks In The Mail, P.O. Box 7802, Irwindale, CA 91706

Clothing

👔 Clean and iron your own clothes.

👔 Avoid clothes that require dry-cleaning.

👔 Wear clothes at least twice before washing and drying.

⚐ Buy plain or neutral color clothes. Solid colors give more combinations than printed.

⚐ Buy clothes cheap, not cheap clothes, especially undergarments.

⚐ Shop garage sales, thrift stores, outlet stores, and discount stores.

⚐ Know sizes for all family members and be ready for a sale.

⚐ Use hand-me-downs.

⚐ Buy clothes on sale and out of season.

⚐ Learn how to dye clothes.

Debt Reduction

▭ Consolidate high interest debts to a lower interest rate.

▭ Call all creditors and ask for a lower rate.

▭ Call all creditors and ask for a waver of any annual fee.

▭ Stop paying with credit cards.

▭ Seek financial advice and consider a home equity loan.

▭ Seek financial advice and consider bankruptcy.

Entertainment

Use discount cards and coupon books. For example, buy a discount dinning card and save up to 25% on your dining bill, or earn frequent flyer miles to help with vacation plans. For someone who has travel and entertainment in their job description, the annual fee ($40 to $100) can be quickly recovered and is a real value. Here are some to consider:

- I Dine: 800-422-5090
  www.idine.com
- Diners Club Card: 800-234-6377
  www.dinersclubus.com
- Dinner on Us Club: 800-346-3241
- Order low-cost specials when dining out.
- Share entrees.
- Go to dollar movies rather than expensive new releases.

Food

- Use coupons.
- Shop alone.
- Don't shop hungry.
- Shop with a list.
- Always compare unit cost when making a purchase (larger quantities are not always cheaper).
- Don't buy products at the end of the isle. (Stores place items at the end of the isle for impulse buying. Chances are there are cheaper brands elsewhere in the store.)
- Ask for rain-checks.
- Shop at stores offering day-old items.
- Join a wholesale club so you can buy bulk.

☞ Buy generic.

☞ Buy seasonal fruits and vegetables.

☞ Don't over-buy perishables.

☞ Read store ads and plan weekly meals around them.

☞ Avoid convenience stores.

☞ Avoid convenience foods.

☞ Cut your own meat and poultry.

☞ Return everything of poor value.

☞ Make your lunch.

☞ Don't eat out.

☞ Grow a garden.

☞ Hunt and fish for food.

Health Care

☞ Consider an HMO or medical coverage with low out-of-pocket deductibles.

☞ Question every medical bill, especially hospital bills.

☞ Consider generic medicine but, ask your doctor first.

☞ Take vitamins.

☞ Exercise regularly.

☞ Have regular check-ups.

☞ Shop by phone for the best price before buying a prescription.

Home

- Take on a roommate or a boarder.

- Refinance your home to a lower interest rate.

- Relocate to lower your cost of living.

- Install an alarm system to lower insurance rates.

- Conserve energy by shutting off lights, air, and heat when not in use.

- Fix leaky faucets and toilets.

- Use a restricted water-saving shower head.

- Close unused rooms.

- Consider average billing for utilities.

- Add insulation, storm windows, solar screens, and other energy conserving products.

- Use fans.

- Use automatic thermostats.

- Do not purchase unnecessary phone services.

- Avoid purchases in season. Don't buy a air conditioner in July.

- Avoid toys that require batteries.

- Use rechargeable batteries.

- Avoid making long distance phone calls.

- Dry clothes outside when possible, or hang damp from the dryer.

Miscellaneous

☞ Shop at pawn shops, newspapers, garage sales, and thrift shops whenever possible.

☞ Use the library rather than purchasing books.

☞ Barter services.

Discipline

When I first heard of Dr. Spock, I thought he was a character on *Star Trek*. Since then, hundreds of psychologists and doctors have written books on the subject of child development and discipline. *Tough Love, Positive Parenting, Discipline with Kindness, Assertive Discipline,* and *Discipline without Spanking, Yelling, Screaming,* or *Pulling Out Hair* have all hit the best sellers' lists. But my father is the expert I learned from.

His lessons resembled those of a dog trainer, but one can't argue with what works. One lesson was communicating through the use of a commanding voice. When my father would say, "Son, time for bed," there was no doubt about what needed to happen. As dog trainers know, the discipline of a dog is a matter of how the dog's master gives commands. My father was an expert at this.

His commands still ring fresh in my mind, and his lessons are priceless. I asked Dad exactly what he did to command the immediate attention and obedience of four children. "If you want a dog to stay off of the couch, don't let him up there as a puppy," he replied. What Dad meant was being consistent with house rules, starting at an early age, communicating the rules, and being prepared to follow through if they are broken. Here are some of his most notable lessons.

There is nothing more annoying than a child who is exhibiting irritating behaviors such as whining, pouting, and throwing temper tantrums. These behaviors need an audience to be effective, and are best handled by ignoring the actions. Dad would say, "Do not give into a child's demands. Simply say, 'I will not listen to you until you can speak calmly and ask in a polite manner.' If that doesn't work, hit them on the nose with a rolled up newspaper." (Or maybe that was for the dog.)

Other behaviors, such as not following rules, not doing chores, refusing to listen, or talking back can be handled the same way. Use a firm voice and tell Junior what is expected. "Stop that now! If you continue with these actions, you will be punished. The choice is yours. What will it be, to be put outside for the night, or be given a biscuit?"

With children involved in day-care, school, or dealing with siblings, name-calling and teasing will surely develop. When this happens, step in with, "Stop! This behavior is not allowed!" Then ask Missy to think how she may feel if she was being picked on and explain how words can hurt others' feelings. (And if this doesn't work, use your slipper on her tail end.)

Along with name-calling generally goes biting, kicking, spitting, and fighting. Immediately stop any physical aggression and again step in with, "Stop! This behavior is not allowed!" Then ask the child to think how she may feel if she was being picked on. If this doesn't work, slap a rolled up newspaper in your hand.

Dad used these methods on our family and I used the same techniques on mine. They are successful for everyday behavioral problems. Start with intervention and a command correcting the inappropriate behavior. My favorite is, "Stop that now! This behavior is not acceptable!" A very important part of being commanding is remaining calm. Yelling does not work. If a father starts yelling, the child wins. Remember, stay in control. Don't be dragged into an argument with a child.

If maintaining self-control is difficult, try counting backwards from 100, take a few minutes away from everyone, breathe, and relax. Once under control, talk to your children about their actions (and listen, too). Such talk could include, "Someone could be hurt, or it is dangerous to play near the street," or other logical points. Dad also suggests "scratching their belly on a regular basis," with praise for following directions: "Thank you for cleaning your room without being asked. I appreciate it very much." Or, "I'm so proud of you."

The last step, if reasoning and discussing a child's misbehavior doesn't work, is punishment. I still remember being scared of my father, but I can't remember him ever hitting me. Dad says, "Spanking doesn't work. If you kick a dog enough, he'll never come to you." Hitting teaches children they are bad and that violent behavior is an acceptable way to express feelings, solve problems, and handle their anger. One shouldn't be surprised if, after using violent punishments raising children, they grow up and strike their spouse. In addition, hitting a child will not correct the behavior problem and can lead to physical and emotional pain.

Dad's favorite punishment was time-out. I think my dad invented this technique and everyone copied him. He would put us in our room, isolated from each other, no games, TV, radio, or any source of entertainment for five to ten minutes at a time. Pure hell! I remember as a child how Dad would calmly explain the conduct that was expected, and if we disobeyed, we were invited to sit in our room. If we would delay taking our appropriate seat, our time-out would be extended for the same amount of time we delayed. He timed us, and pleas of, "Can I get out now?" only added time to the sentence. I could hear the kitchen timer from fifty paces and longed for the buzzer to go off. But the best part was how he was there after each time-out to talk and say, "Punishing you hurts me more than it does you." (You know, I never did believe that part of it.)

But my father's best lesson came with his actions, lessons in life, everyday. I wonder if he realizes how his honest, caring and loving guidance has led me to who I am today. He was noble in showing me that discipline was more than correcting a child through the use of punishment. Discipline is an everyday lesson on ethics and morality. A father has a responsibility to his children, himself, and society to model appropriate behavior, teach right from wrong, and instill basic values of self-respect and pride. This is a parent's responsibility, not the school's, church's, or sitter's. "Our world would be a wonderful place if we all lived by the Golden Rule, 'Do unto others as you would have them do unto you,'" he said. And the best way to teach a child this is by example. Dad, I learned from the best.

Discipline And The Split Household

My father was married for 49 years before my mother passed away. He never had to deal with disciplining a child between two different homes, or enforcing a restriction when his children went to visit Mom. Nor did he have to enforce discipline during his visitation periods as a non-custodial parent or have to deal with a child filled with resentment and anger from an ugly divorce. I had to learn these lessons the hard way.

One hopes that a father's selection of his children's mother was someone who shares his values. If Mom and Dad want Junior to do well in school, it will be much easier to work out solutions to behavior problems concerning grades. However, if Mom thinks her daughter should be allowed to smoke at age 14 and Dad disagrees, there will be much conflict.

I remember my parents occasionally disagreeing on discipline. The chances of two parents from any household agreeing on house rules, family values, discipline procedures, and punishments are not great. So expecting to have a completely agreeable and workable co-parenting relationship regarding discipline is highly unrealistic. A custodial father who expects his children to follow his rules in Mom's house during visitation periods, or who plans on being unsupportive of a custodial parent by foregoing necessary discipline, is setting himself up for a great disappointment.

Exchanging periods of custody can be challenging when trying to enforce a child's restrictions, and can often lead to a punishment that goes unenforced in the other home. The easiest way around this is allowing punishments to finish before children visit Mom. This way children and Mom are able to enjoy their time together. If this is not possible, inform Mom of the circumstances that led to the punishment and what restriction was used as a penalty. Then ask for her support by implementing a restriction that she feels is appropriate and enforceable.

But just because a punishment fits one household, doesn't mean the same restriction will suit the other. For instance, if I restrict one of my children from the Internet and Mom doesn't have a computer, there isn't much of a punishment. Or, if I move bedtime to 8:00 P.M. and Mom doesn't finish homework and dinner until 8:30, the punishment is unenforceable and worthless.

However, Mom may find other means of punishment that are more suited to her household. It is important to allow non-custodial parents to be parents in their own home. And of course, the same holds true when roles are reversed.

Another situation my father missed was putting children on restriction with punishments that wouldn't punish him. If Dad said there was no TV after dinner and bedtime was at eight, he didn't have to be there to enforce the penalty. Mom was around to help. Some of my favorite hands-off punishments are:

▲ Restrictions: Take away favorite toys, video games, and privileges.

▲ Writing: Have a child write spelling words, homework, the dictionary, or a story on his punishment.

▲ Doing chores: My house is always cleanest when my kids have misbehaved! I use vacuuming, cleaning, cutting the grass, washing the car or dishes, or a variety of other domestic chores as punishments.

As single parents, we sometimes find it easier to allow our children to go unpunished for inappropriate behavior because we don't want to risk re-igniting hatred or anger carried over from the family separation. But a single parent must discipline his children and make them know the consequences of their inappropriate actions. Disciplining a child as a single parent can also help strengthen the co-parent relationship by not sending spoiled brats back to the custodial parent to correct. (And, of course, the same holds true when roles are reversed.)

Affordable Family Time

ary's wife left Texas with his children and later filed for divorce and custody in another state. Unable to appear on his own behalf or afford an attorney, the court ordered Gary to pay child support in what amounted to 49 percent of his take-home pay. But eventually, Gary's ex-wife and kids returned to Dallas, and Gary could barely contain his excitement over his first visit. He said, "I'm taking my kids to Chuck E Cheese tonight," as though it was a trip to Disneyland.

Gary is a loving father and is very active in his children's lives. He must work part-time jobs just to make ends meet, so when his children visit on weekends he can't afford to be a "Disneyland Dad." He has mastered the art of family entertainment at affordable prices. "When my kids come to visit, they get bored in my small apartment. Video games will only hold their attention for a short time, and when you live on a budget as tight as mine, 10 bucks is substantial, 20 is splurging." Here are some of Gary's affordable entertainment tips:

- Make arts and crafts
- Play board games such as checkers, chess, Monopoly, cards, and so on
- Play basketball games such as Horse or Around the World
- Picnic in the park
- Play catch with a baseball, football, frisbee
- Make a puzzle or model
- Go to dollar movie or rent a video
- Visit the library
- Go swimming at community pool, apartment pool, or local lakes
- Go fishing
- Go hiking
- Plant a garden
- Play indoor or outdoor putt-putt

- Have water fun with a hose and sprinkler or water balloons

- Fly a kite

- Camp out in the back yard

- Make a snowman or go sledding, followed by hot chocolate

- Call the local parks and recreation department for a schedule of free events

- Visit the zoo, or other cultural facilities such as children's museums

- Visit friends and family

- Visit fast food restaurants with play places

- Visit batting cages

- Visit flea markets, thrift shops, and dollar stores

- Go to free concerts

- Go to high school sporting events, theaters, and musical productions

- Go bicycling or walking, using a reward such as visiting an ice-cream stand for the final destination

Andrew, like Gary, lives on a limited income. His secret to affordable family time is giving time rather than gifts. "I try to take advantage of every minute I have with my child. My standard visitation order says I have possession of my son from Wednesday after school to Thursday morning and the first, third, and fifth weekends." For Andrew, every minute with his son is quality time. "I use the time in the morning for us to talk as we get ready together. My son even likes to shave with me. After school is for exercise and doing homework; evenings end with a bedtime story."

In addition to court-ordered time, Andrew's ex-wife is flexible with visitation. "My son calls me when there is a school project due, and I even take him with me when I run errands. He loves to go with me when I pick up supplies for my contracting business."

Andrew also avoids the TV. He says, "Good conversation and the TV go together like oil and water. Besides, I think the television turns my son's brain to mush." Andrew has house rules on watching TV. Number one, no TV during dinner. Number two, TV is allowed only after doing something meaningful or that has a purpose. "I make him draw, read, or exercise before watching TV." Number three, if home work isn't done, the tube is off. According to Andrew, the best part of limited television is how much more active he is with his son. "We ride bikes, play catch, and swim as often as we can. I don't even have cable TV anymore. I'm saving money and I have a terrific relationship with my son because we are not stuck to the tube."

Doug, a visiting parent of two, insists on having plans every weekend. "I want my children to know when they come to my apartment that we won't just be watching TV." Doug takes advantage of community papers for free or low-cost entertainment. "We go everywhere: coin shows, art shows, and concerts for free or low cost." Most local papers have a section where they list a calendar of events for the arts, museums, music, recreation, workshops, readings and lectures, sports, and theater activities. Admission prices, if any, are normally listed; or a simple phone call can uncover quality entertainment for little or no cost. Doug also notes, "There is a different type of woman found at museums than at night-clubs."

Paul uses sports for his quality time. "Sports are a big part of my children's lives. My daughter plays soccer and my son plays baseball." The key to sports is involvement and encouragement. "I go to as many practices as I can, and it takes a natural disaster to keep me from a game. There are even times I watch half of my son's game and half of my daughter's at two different locations." Paul also suggests being supportive and offering tips in a positive way. "Don't make children feel bad for lack of talent or mistakes they make. I try not to be upset when my son isn't the best one on the field or when my daughter makes a mistake. After all, they are trying the best they can."

One other benefit of being active in his children's sporting events has been the attention Andrew receives from the players' moms. "They are always trying to fix me up with someone. Being a good dad sure has its advantages."

John, a custodial father of two, tries to include emotional support during his time with his children. He claims giving consistent love is the key to family time. "My children are growing and developing their own lives and social agenda. They have their own friends and school activities and are always on the go. This makes it difficult to maintain an open and honest relationship with them. We are not always in the house at the same time.

"My biggest concern is that I get wrapped up in my work or domestic responsibilities, and sometimes forget to give my children the time they need and deserve. So, I have a house rule that dinner is always served at the table. This really provides time for us to talk. The way I figure it, kids are like dogs. When they are hungry, they'll come home. And when they do, I'm there.

"I know a lot about my children because of this. I know who their best friends are, what classes they are taking, and what was the last movie they saw. This is the foundation to open communication.

"I also spend a little time with each child individually and make an effort to hold and love them. When my kids were babies, I would crawl on the ground with them and make those stupid baby sounds. Today I'm lucky to have 10 to 15 minutes of quiet time with them and maybe put my arm around them."

John also has a philosophy about saying good-bye. "I never let the last words out of my mouth be negative or cruel, even if we have been arguing. I just couldn't imagine some thing terrible happening to me or my children and my last words are anything but, 'I love you.'"

One last note on affordable family time. Place the emphasis on *family*, not *affordable*. Understandably, spending money to go places is not always possible, but family time is every where and everyday. It is at school programs, while talking on the phone, teaching children your trade, doing house chores, or building things. Involvement is the key.

Dress Well for Less

I wasn't always a bad dresser. There was a time when I looked pretty damn good for any occasion. I never worried about what shirt matched what pants, what was in style, or when clothes needed to be replaced. Women used to turn to look at me. But, that was a few years ago, when my wife dressed me. I'm not ashamed to admit it: she selected my clothes. Hell, what was I to do? She would say, "Honey, I like to dress you and make other women jealous." Hard to believe there was a time this actually made sense, but I let her dress me anyway. Besides, I never enjoyed shopping for clothes.

Now, I'm not sure exactly when I realized my wardrobe was in trouble. It might have been the day I walked by a full length mirror wearing black socks, sandals, cutoffs, and a Buffalo Bills T-shirt, or it could have been the time I was mistaken for a Wal-Mart employee. I guess it was about three or four years after my divorce. You know, the time it takes to *grow* through a wardrobe.

Dave, a custodial father of two, realized his style needed help three years after his divorce when he was accused of stealing clothes from a thrift store. He said, "During my marriage, my wife hung my shirts, pants, and ties together for me. Fashion decisions were never part of my routine."

Millions of other divorced men have found themselves in the same situation. Let's meet some and share their wardrobe dilemmas and solutions.

Tony, divorced for two years, discovered his fashion was in trouble when his kids laughed at him for wearing socks pulled up to his knees. He recalls, "When I divorced, I started dressing myself and found myself in trouble. Then I met Jasmine. She looked and acted like a super model. On our first date she made me promise never to wear anything from a list she gave me or she wouldn't go out with me again." Here's the list:

✗   Socks with sandals

✗   White shoes

✗ Pants that show your butt crack

✗ Pants pulled up too high

✗ Short pants

✗ Leisure suits

✗ Knee-high socks with shorts

✗ Shorts with a long sleeve shirt

✗ A tie with a short sleeve shirt

✗ Blue or any other color hair

✗ Pocket protectors

✗ Short shorts

✗ Suspenders and shorts

✗ Sunglasses or tinted glasses while in doors

✗ Dirty ball caps

✗ Tucking in a tie or wearing short ties that don't reach your belt

✗ Tie tacks or clips

✗ Plaids with stripes or checks

✗ A belt and suspenders at the same time

✗ Speedos

✗ A watch with a calculator on it

✗ Underwear with holes

✗ T-shirts that don't cover your belly (unless you can wash clothes on your stomach)

- ✗ A wallet on a chain
- ✗ Keychains hanging full of keys
- ✗ Loafers and shorts
- ✗ Boots with dress pants
- ✗ Red socks
- ✗ Short socks
- ✗ Boots and shorts
- ✗ A comb across or a bad hairpiece

"On our second date she gave me another list. This one was on the subtleties of fashion. She said, 'Do these things if you ever expect any of *this*,' as she ran her hand over her hour glass figure."

- ✓ If you need to ask, "Does this need to be ironed?", it does
- ✓ No holes in your clothes
- ✓ Don't eat with a hat on
- ✓ Wear clean shoes
- ✓ Always wear a belt if your pants have loops
- ✓ Socks should match pants
- ✓ Shave everyday
- ✓ Shower everyday
- ✓ No nose hair

✓ Exercise

✓ Keep nails clean and trimmed

✓ Keep facial hair trimmed, this includes eyebrows

✓ Keep hair (any length) clean and neat

"Now, you may be thinking, 'What a prissy bitch! Who would want to put up with that attitude just for a piece of ass?' Me too! But I did keep to the lists."

Stephen, divorced six years, worked in a laboratory. For the most part, he wore boots, jeans, and a sport shirt. Riding by on his Harley, hair in a pony tail, wearing a leather vest, he didn't appear to be at the cutting edge of technology. Well, Stephen needed to attend a large formal company function to kiss a little ass for a new piece of equipment he wanted (something to do with saving the world I think) and he needed to purchase his first suit.

As the story goes, Stephen now wears a suit regularly and has acquired the art of buying quality that fits a tight budget, too. "I'm not ashamed to say cheap. I can't pay more for a suit than I do for child support. I must know how to dress for less," he says. "I have several suits I paid less than a hundred bucks for that I can wear to any board meeting." Here are some of his secrets:

> Never buy a suit that is not on sale. Paying list price is foolish, especially if the suit is only worn a few times each year. Besides, it doesn't hurt as much when you spill coffee or get grease on it when you are pumping gas.

> ❯ Shop at second-hand stores. Not Goodwill or the Salvation Army, but consignment stores of the rich and desperate. Most suits have enough fabric (two inches or less) to make small alterations.

> ❯ Go to garage sales in up-scale neighborhoods.

> ❯ Shop at close-out and outlet stores while following this guideline: Nothing in the store is worth more than $200, that's why it's there.

Stephen also admits that shopping for price can lead to trouble and shares another important secret when selecting a suit: the fit. "I'd be the first to admit, I can't tell the difference between a suit from K-Mart or one from Armani without reading the tag, but I can tell when someone looks like ten pounds of dirt in a five pound bag." Stephen shares the advice he received from John J.T. Terry, wardrobe consultant for the Men's Warehouse in Arlington, Texas, on fitting a suit:

> ◎ The first choice when buying a suit is color. Stay with something corporate such as gray, blue, or black for your first three suits. These are commonly considered "power suits" and appropriate for almost everything. Avoid bold patterns and colors.

> ◎ Next, consider the material. Wool is the most desirable fabric, and the higher the thread count (80, 90, 100, super 100) the more durable and the smoother the appearance.

◎ Now try on the jacket over the shirt that will be worn. Stand in front of a three-way mirror and examine the fit with the jacket buttoned.

◎ The collar of the jacket should hug the back of your neck with no gap.

◎ The back of the jacket should fall smoothly and follow the curve of your back with no vertical creases, especially in the shoulder area.

◎ The vent(s) in the back should not pull open when you are standing erect and the length of the jacket should cover the seat of your trousers.

◎ The waistline of the jacket should conform to your own waistline comfortably with room to move.

◎ When buttoned, the front of the jacket should lie flat across your chest and the buttons should line up.

◎ Sleeve length should be the point where the hand meets the wrist. (Be sure to check both sleeves, as most people have one arm longer than the other.)

◎ Next, try on the trousers with the shoes that will be worn.

◎ Make sure that the trousers fit comfortably around your waist. The pockets, pleats, and zipper should lie flat without bulges.

◎ Creases should be clearly visible from the bottom of the pocket all the way down.

◎   The break in the pants should be at the top of the shoe.

◎   The length should be long enough to cover your socks when you walk without stepping on the cuff.

Robert, divorced for six years, thought buying his own clothes would be easy. He said, "How hard can shopping be if women enjoy doing it?" In a short time he found himself looking like a 60's flashback and realized staying in style is the key to looking good. He now recommends the following:

❋   Visit popular or trendy clothing stores such as the Gap or Structure, and look at the combinations they have on display. Window shop.

❋   If you can afford to, buy something from these stores. However, don't buy items that will be covered up by an outer layer. Make sure the name brand logo is visible.

❋   Ask the sales clerk for other combinations, colors that would look good with your purchase, or colors that would look good on you. Some people need help with this. This is a good way to buy accessories, such as T-shirts, from other stores at lower prices.

❋   Read articles on current fashion in men's magazines such as *Men's Health, Maxim,* and *Gentleman's Quarterly.* In addition, look at the style men are wearing in the advertisements.

❋   Look around and see what well-dressed men are wearing. People watch.

Lou, divorced for two years, had difficulty selecting footwear for all of his different dress requirements. "I wear a suit to meetings, business casual around the office, western wear at the honky-tonk, and casual clothes anytime else. Luckily my neighbor, Joel Parker is the store director from Larry's Shoes in Arlington, Texas, and assembled the following guidelines for me."

* Regarding color, black shoes match attire which is black, navy, and various shades of gray; brown shoes match dark brown, tan, olive, beige, and khaki; cordovan goes with blue, navy, gray, and earth tones.

* Always buy leather.

* Keep shoes clean and shined.

* For business dress, wear medallions, wing tips, oxfords, monk straps, or tassel loafers. No boots, penny loafers, or athletic shoes. For casual, business casual, and western attire stick with loafers (penny loafers are still a safe choice), oxfords, cowboy boots, or hiking boots.

* Give your socks some thought, too. They should match your pants. Wear something besides black, especially with jeans. Try varieties of color and patterns and make sure socks are long enough that there is no skin showing when sitting down.

* Belts should match shoes and should be darker than your clothes, leather, between 1¼ and 1½ inches wide, long enough to reach the first loop in your pants, and with a simple buckle.

Mac, divorced for nine years, sums up men's style like this: "Fashion is not just what you wear to work or to a club, it's what you wear every time you leave your house. Single men should always be ready meet Ms. Right and never go out thinking it doesn't matter what you look like. The one time you go to the mailbox looking like a geek, Ms. Right will be there, and there is no second chance for a first impression."

What about the kids?

Dave, divorced for six months, recalls, "I wore a uniform to work and my casual clothes were in good shape. But, with four children in different age groups, my problem was dressing my kids at an affordable price."

Dave quickly learned that different aged children presented different challenges when it came to clothes. Infants don't care what they wear. They spend most of their time under blankets or in a one-piece suit. Buying clothes for this age is simple, as clothes are commonly sold in sets that take the guesswork out of coordinating colors. The biggest problem dressing infants to age three is that children are either spitting up or spilling something, and stains on new clothes are like throwing away money. "At this age, I really try to avoid buying anything new," Dave said. "I rely on secondhand stores and hand-me-downs."

Sometime around the age of three or four, children try to dress themselves. The focus on selecting their clothing should be to help them gain independence by selecting clothes that make dressing easy. Avoid clothes and shoes that require buttons, zippers, and ties. Use a large selection of solid colors so they can select their own clothes, and try to buy clothes with pictures on the front to make it easy for them to know what side goes where. "Elastic and Velcro are staples in my children's wardrobe," Dave explains.

Children around the ages of 8 to 16 have a good idea of what they want to wear. As a result, cost and differing views on what's appropriate can cause major stress in a house hold. "My oldest daughter and I really got into it because I wouldn't allow her to wear all black. My goodness, she looked like death," said Dave.

After age 16 a child should be encouraged to work for his/her own wardrobe. "I help my son out at holidays, birthdays, and special occasions by buying him clothes, but most purchases he makes himself," Dave adds.

Regardless of the age, the only way many fathers can afford to dress children is to save money when buying clothes. Here are Dave's best cost-cutters:

- ✩ Use hand-me-downs; not just from your family, but also previously worn clothes swapped with other parents. This helps tremendously when it comes to jeans, shoes, and play clothes.

- ✩ Always carry your children's sizes and be ready for a sale or close-out.

- ✩ Never buy clothes that don't allow for growth.

- ✩ Avoid buying clothes that are not on sale.

☆ Shop at secondhand stores.

☆ Go to garage sales in up-scale neighborhoods.

☆ Avoid clothes that require dry-cleaning.

☆ Shop at close-out and outlet stores.

☆ Wear clothes at least twice before washing and drying.

☆ Buy plain or neutral color clothes.

☆ Solid colors give more combinations than printed.

☆ Buy clothes cheap, not cheap clothes, especially under-garments.

☆ Shop at discount stores.

☆ Learn how to dye clothes.

☆ Avoid seasonal purchases.

☆ Share clothes between family members.

Finding Mrs. Right II

More than twenty years ago we met as The Women Haters' Club. Today, with a slightly different agenda, we reconvene. (Who would have thought we would outgrow that time of youth?) Our mission for this meeting is not to plan a water balloon attack on Suzie, but to gain an advantage on the female race. This time we want to know everything. Where to find them, how to ask them out, how to please them, and how to afford them. Most of all, we want to be smarter than them. So, at this board meeting we intend to share our years of experience and our never before told secrets. The way we figure, when we are through, no woman will be safe.

Before we convene, let me introduce our board members. First, there's Russ. We once called him the Italian Stallion. Russ was the type of guy who was so good-looking, no matter how he treated women, they couldn't stay away. Today, Russ is a divorced parent in his second marriage. **This time** to the girl of his dreams.

Next, there is Randy. As a young man we called him Candy Randy. Not because he was a sissy, but because so many women were sweet on him. He had an irresistible smile, a baby face, and he loved to compete with Russ. Today, Randy is a typical visiting parent and takes a love 'em and leave 'em attitude, bitter from trusting his former wife.

Then there's Jerry. In high school, Jerry dated Donna, the hottest babe in town. To look at Jerry, one might say, "Donna is way too good-looking for him." (Well, at least we thought so.) Then we all went skinny-dipping and figured it out. Back then, Jerry didn't want to jeopardize his relationship with Donna, so he operated like a commando when he was allowed his monthly night out with the boys. He had girl-friends in five surrounding counties. Today he is still dating Donna. That's right, for more than 20 years they have been dating. They have a little girl now, and Jerry still goes out with the boys once a month.

Then there's me. In my youth, I was Mr. Average. According to Russ and Randy, "Mr. Nice Guy, too nice," they'd say. But, by hanging out with such competition, I was forced to compensate with brains and charm. (Okay, some might call it BS). Today, by choice, I am a happy, single, custodial father of three.

What makes this bunch the experts? Well, with the exception of the grunge period we went through, we have always had a female companion. Besides, who else to give practical advice about women? Dr. Geek?

Tonight we set up the card table without cards and chips. Instead, we bring books, magazines, and note pads. I volunteer to take the minutes and the meeting is called to order at 8:05 P.M.

When to start dating?

"When is it appropriate to begin dating after divorce?" drowns the echo from the gavel. "Yeah, what about the children?"

We all agree that dating should start when it feels right, and this time frame depends greatly on the relationship that just ended. I personally could not start dating for almost a year after my divorce, while some members (names withheld) were actually dating while they were still married.

Our confusion (and guilt) comes from entertaining in front of our children. What do you say the first time you have an overnight guest, start locking your door at night, or have a stranger at the breakfast table?

We agree that our wanting companionship is healthy, natural, and critical for a child's positive development. We also agree that we ***deserve to be happy!*** But, when a child sees Dad with someone other than Mom, it can be a traumatic experience, especially the first time. (One only needs to hear a child cry once about Dad dating to learn this lesson.) Randy says, "I never enjoy lying to my children about dating, but before introducing them to anyone new, I go on three or four dates with her. Why should I complicate my children's lives by involving them with someone that I just don't see myself with in the future?"

Randy adds, "The best thing I ever did to make dating easier was setting time aside for my own social life immediately after my divorce. When my personal time was slowly shared with another adult, my children easily adapted."

> To help ease the awkwardness of meeting Dad's new girlfriend, don't meet at home. Try an entertaining setting like miniature golf or a fast-food restaurant like McDonald's. This puts everyone on neutral ground, and the atmosphere holds fun and excitement.

New Sleeping Arrangements

Next, we want some guidelines on sleeping with a new girlfriend. Specifically, "When we can expect to rumble in the sheets?" Our answer is concise: sex is most likely to happen on the third to fifth date.

Randy shares his sure-fire agenda to make this happen. "Take her to a nice hotel in a nearby town on the third date. Be prepared with candles, grapes, strawberries, cheese, french bread, chocolate, lubricants, whatever you need to create a loving atmosphere. A well-planned hotel visit is a sure way to get laid."

SPECIAL NOTE: *One of us mentioned an incident when he paid for airfare and hotel accommodations, only to have his date say, "Just 'cause we are in a different town doesn't automatically mean I'm going to sleep with you." (We all agreed this is a waste of good airfare.)*

Finding Miss Right

The next item on the agenda has been bothering us for some time: where does one find a good woman? Russ says, "Hunting for a mate is like finding a favorite wine. One must sample several bottles."

"That's great," we note, "but some of us have a difficult time just finding a date." "That's because you don't look in the right places, or you're sitting on your ass," Russ says. "Women aren't in the car behind you as you drive from work. You have to be where they are." Here are Russ's best and worst places to meet women:

Best Places To Meet Women

  Children's school and sports functions.

  Amusement parks.

  Libraries.

  Adult education or lessons of any kind.

  Restaurants (unless she's the waitress).

  Coffee shops.

- Bookstores.

- Record stores.

- Parties.

- Happy hours.

- Parks.

- Vacation spots.

- Health clubs.

- Sporting events.

- Exhibit shows and museums.

- Church groups.

- Weddings (not yours).

- Grocery stores and malls.

- Fast food restaurants (especially on Saturday and Sunday morning).

- Any place you enjoy being away from home

- ALSO NOTED: It helps to ask friends, neighbors, family and co-workers if they know anyone who may be available. Just make sure not to sound like you're asking for pity.

Worst Places To Meet Women

- Home improvement centers.

- Personal ads.

- Dating and matchmaking services.

- Single's clubs and bars.

- Any place that requires wearing a name tag.

- Any "anonymous" program.

- Work.

- 900 numbers.

- Gentlemen's clubs.

- Adult video stores.

- Blind dates.

- On the web.

- From a catalog.

What to say?

Meeting women face-to-face brought us to our next subject of what to say and do when we finally see someone we would like to meet. After all, staring only goes so far. Jerry (Mr. Commando), operating under a time restraint, claims to be an expert on this topic and offers the following strategies and cautions:

"The most important part of breaking down the barrier when meeting a woman is making the incident seem coincidental and inevitable. Simply adapting your approach to the setting at hand is a sure win."

He uses a scene from *My Blue Heaven* as example. Vinnie, played by Steve Martin, meets Shaldeen, played by Carol Kane, standing in front of an open freezer door at the grocery store.

Vinnie says, "You know, it's dangerous for you to be here in the frozen foods section."

"Why's that?" Shaldeen replies.

"Because you could melt all diss stuff."

Jerry also points out that 80 percent of success in meeting women comes from how one carries himself. "If you carry yourself with modesty, confidence, sensitivity, and have a sense of humor, women will at least talk to you."

ALSO NOTED: *Don't buy a book on pick-up lines. They only tell you what not to say and make advances looked rehearsed and scripted. We share our worst attempts at pick-up lines:*

✘   What's your sign?

✘   Is it hot in here, or is it just you?

✘   Come here often?

✘   Are your legs tired? (Why?) Because you have been running through my mind all day.

✘   I lost my number. Can I have yours?

✘   My face is leaving in ten minutes and I'd like you on it.

✘   Do you wash your pants in glass cleaner? (No, why?) Because I can see myself in them.

✘   There is only one thing that would look better on you than that dress. (What?) Me!

Jerry continues by saying, "The other 20 percent is what you say. Simply say hello and introduce yourself. Then let simple conversation follow. Try to find a common interest, ask open-ended questions, and at some point give her an honest compliment. If she has children with her, make a nice comment about them. Chicks dig guys who like kids."

ALSO NOTED: *Using her name immediately in conversation and when saying good-bye is very effective.*

Miscellaneous (and a little Folklore)

Now, Jerry gave me this advice years ago, and for the most part, it serves me well. But for me, I must have every advantage when I see a woman I'd like to connect with. These are my deepest secrets that help me increase my odds of success:

- 👄 Do not approach a woman if she is wearing a wedding ring. These women are normally married or are wearing the ring to prevent unwanted advances. Either way, odds are against you.

- 👄 While looking at the hands for rings, look for a pinky ring. Women who wear pinky rings always seem to have some sexual preferences that make them great lovers. And if she has two, look out!

- 👄 Next look at the face. According to *The Naked Face* by Lailan Young, there are signs on the face that can help one select a partner. First, the lips: A larger upper lip denotes someone who, under the right circumstances, may be attracted to extra-marital affairs.

💋 Look for a dip at the center of the upper lip, called the point of refinement. When there is a perceptible vertical line joining this point to the bottom of the upper lip its possessor will not only be romantic, but a refined and delicately creative lover.

💋 A larger lower lip indicates someone whose need for love exceeds their ability to love. (Just what I need, another one-sided relationship.) And anyone with a fleshy lower lip will seek physical pleasures in abundance.

💋 Lips of equal size indicate someone who is able to give and receive affection in equal amounts.

💋 Thin lips usually belong to someone who is mean and unforgiving, and I personally think they are lousy kissers.

💋 Look for a wide philtrum. This is the vertical groove joining the base of the nose to the upper lip. Anything over a half-an-inch wide, at its widest point, indicates a healthy sexual appetite.

💋 Look for intensely green, blue, or blue-green eyes. This indicates a frantic, creative sexual appetite. (Copyright © 1993, by Lailan Young. From *The Naked Face* by Lailan Young. Reprinted by permission of St. Martin's Press, LLC.)

💋 ALSO NOTED: *The shape or outline of the nose is in direct correlation to the shape of the breast. (Providing there has been no cosmetic surgery, at either end.) A nose that slants up at the end indicates a set of firm, perky breasts. A nose that slants down reveals elliptical breast that will hang with the same outline. We all agreed this has nothing to do with character, but it was the most fun we could have with a nose.*

Next, we combine our personal experiences and conclude that each age group of women is different. We find women in their twenties are sexually experimental and this makes it easier to educate or liberate them. Younger women are also quick to commit and love to be in a relationship. In their thirties women become sexually aware, and at some point between the late thirties and early forties reach their sexual peak. (How fair is this?) From there estrogen levels drop, and once women hit their fifties, they (as we expect to be) are as grateful as hell.

Asking For A Date

Next on the agenda is asking for a date. We summarize by saying, "If you are going to ask a woman out, you better have a plan. At least a simple one. Show that there has been some thought behind asking her. A woman wants to feel that she is special."

Never ask for a first date without giving her ample notice. Many women will not accept a date for Friday after Wednesday. They rationalize, "I will not be someone's last ditch effort to get a date."

Going on a first date made all of us question how to get a second date. The overall consensus is to act like a gentleman, carry a conversation, and don't whine. When the date is near an end, and if you like her, **ask to see her again.** However, we want to share our favorite signs that a date is going nowhere and when just saying goodnight is appropriate. The date is in trouble if she:

- Frequently looks at her watch.
- Says, "You're a nice guy, but . . ."
- Flirts with other men.
- Says, "You won't get mad if I dance with him, will you?"
- Compares you to her ex-husband or boyfriend.
- Says, "I'm tired."
- Calls you by the wrong name.
- Says, "I just want to be friends," or "I don't know if I'm ready for a relationship."
- Says, "I have to work early tomorrow."
- Says, "I'm a lesbian."

Affordable Dates

"How can we go on all these dates and manage a family budget when a guy is expected to pay on the first date?" is the next topic open for discussion.

Russ points out, "A date doesn't have to cost big bucks to be fun. A cheap date is the solution to a *guy always having to pay.*"

We all agreed and came up with suggestions for dating on a family budget:

- ☺ Exercise in the park.
- ☺ Play tennis.
- ☺ Go to a drive-in (if she doesn't mind riding in the trunk).
- ☺ Go to a lake.
- ☺ Watch the sun go down.
- ☺ Find or build a fire at the beach, woods, or home. There's something about a fire that is relaxing and hypnotic.
- ☺ Look at the stars.
- ☺ Go to a party.
- ☺ Rent a movie.
- ☺ Have dinner at home.
- ☺ Visit friends.
- ☺ Walk your dog.
- ☺ Picnic in the park.
- ☺ Visit the zoo.
- ☺ Visit the museum/planetarium/arboretum.
- ☺ Go to an antique store or shows.
- ☺ Go to a craft store or shows.
- ☺ Walk downtown.

☺   Attend a church activity or service.

☺   Watch a dollar movie.

☺   Go to a car show.

☺   *It's best to go somewhere familiar on a first date. This allows you to operate under comfortable and controlled conditions, giving her a sense of security.*

Serious Dating

Although we agree that sex alone does not constitute a relationship, intimacy is *normally* a sign you're on your way. So, the next focus of our group is trying to figure out at what point women think you are committed. We conclude you are in a relationship if you:

❤   Don't mind taking her to a dirty bedroom.

❤   Don't shower before a date.

❤   Wear socks with holes in them.

❤   Fart or burp with glee.

❤   Don't button your pants when she visits.

❤   Have your pictures taken together.

❤   Don't have to ask her if she is busy on Friday.

❤   Have feminine napkins in your house.

❤   Have a section of your medicine cabinet just for her stuff.

❤   Have her clothes in your closet.

- 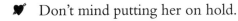 Don't mind putting her on hold.

- Say, "I love you."

- Use nicknames such as "honey" or "sweetums".

- Have a "joint" anything.

- Stop taking her clothes off.

- Have sex often (with the same woman).

Because it is so easy to go from, "Will you call me?" to "Where were you last night?" we (with the exception of Jerry) think it is best to avoid starting a relationship with someone who is realistically incompatible. For example:

Randy will not date anyone *without* children. He says, "Women without parental responsibilities do not understand when there is a *slight inconvenience* associated with parenting. This adds too much stress to a relationship." He recalls one such incident, "I dated a girl who got mad when I wouldn't leave my son alone to ride a roller coaster with her. After that I felt uncomfortable every time we included my son in our plans." Russ, on the other hand, says, "After my divorce, I wouldn't date anyone *with* children. I was a visiting parent and loved my freedom. Now don't get me wrong, I would have loved to be with my son more than every other weekend, but my "ex" was never going to let that happen. So, my time was exactly that. I traveled and was always on the go. The last thing I wanted was to be tied down by someone else's children. That would be unhealthy for all involved."

My difficulty is being in a relationship with a woman who has two or more children. That may sound selfish coming from a father of three, but living like the Brady Bunch is not appealing to me.

Jerry says, "You're all too damn picky. No wonder you don't get laid!"

When sex was brought up, we all wanted to share the secrets of pleasing a woman. Here are our favorites, in no particular order:

- Send her flowers. Not just any flowers. Roses.
- Caress her by touching or kissing her softly on any soft skin such as inside the thighs, behind the knees, stomach, genitals, the neck, ears, and breasts.
- ALSO NOTED: *None of us know the exact way to stimulate a woman's breasts. Russ shares his frustration, "I dated this girl who loved it when I pinched and bit her nipples. So the next girl I was with got the same treatment. To my surprise, she slapped me and said, 'What the hell are you doing? That hurts.' Hell, I'm afraid to touch them anymore!"*
- Give her a massage.
- One member describes each woman having a threshold to her sexual comfort. The secret of being a good lover is finding where this line is, and pushing it ever so slightly.
- Long, meaningful kisses.

🌿 Another member found a very special service called the *Panty-of-the-Month* that adds fire to his relationship. Each month he sends (via the service) a designer panty, perfumed, gift-wrapped, and enclosed with a personal note to his girlfriend's doorstep. He claims this is a real turn-on, well at least for him. (The rest of us scrambled to write down the 24-hour information hotline, (515)469-6800, or www.panties.com).

🌿 The same member also suggested purchasing a copy of *101 Nights of Grrreat Sex* by Laura Corn (Park Ave. Press, 1995). The book contains 101 sealed envelopes, each with suggestions for seduction, half for you and half for her. ALSO NOTED: Only one woman per book.

🌿 Love her. Desire her.

🌿 *Foreplay, foreplay, foreplay, foreplay, foreplay.*

🌿 Have quicky sex. Anytime, anyplace. In a parking lot, during lunch, in a car, or any where the mood strikes.

🌿 Talk during sex. (Not about the weather.)

🌿 Watch an adult video.

🌿 Give and receive oral sex.

🌿 ALSO NOTED: Never pull her ears or push her head down.

🌿 Make some noise. Don't just lie there with your eyes closed.

🌿 Stimulate her clitoris. This is the small pink organ located where the inner vagina lips meet at the top of the vaginal opening.

🌱 Discover her "G" spot. This is the small mass of tissue located inside the vagina approximately one-third of the way up the front wall. To locate her "G" spot, push gently along the wall of the vagina (palm up, fingers bent slightly) until you find a slightly rougher, somewhat ribbed patch of roundish skin. This sensitive place can produce a climax through intercourse or other methods of stimulation.

🌱 ALSO NOTED: *Some women prefer to be on top or have rear entry during intercourse to find this spot. And never ask a women, "Was it good for you?" If you have to ask, it probably wasn't.*

We have quite a list going and asked what sources of information were the most helpful. We all agree that there are two books on this subject that every man should read. They are:

🕯 *How to Make Love All Night (and Drive a Woman Wild)* by Barbara Keesling, Ph.D. (Prima Publishing, 1995) teaches how to prolong love-making by strengthening the "PC" muscle. (That's the muscle you feel when you try to stop urinating.) Dr. Keesling explains how men can:

> Have orgasms without losing your erection
>
> Have orgasms before ejaculating
>
> Have multiple orgasms just like a woman
>
> Have longer lasting, more intense orgasms

🕯 *Drive Your Women Wild In Bed: A Lover's Guide To Sex and Romance* by Stacy Keith (The Time Warner Company,

1994), filled with hundreds of ways to please a women. To name a few:

Advice on everything from spanking to toys

Women's fantasies

Fail-proof techniques to bring her to orgasm every time

How to overcome the fear of rejection

How to buy lingerie she will love

🖈 And for those who prefer to watch rather than read, there is *The Better Sex Video Series,* by the Sinclair Institute, Dept. 8PB53, P.O. Box 8865, Chapel Hill, NC 27517, (800)955-0888, ext. 8PB53, www.bettersex.com. This series offers sexually explicit educational videos with explanations and advice from nationally recognized sex therapists.

Although we are all comfortable with our manhood, we can't help feeling a little uncomfortable shopping for sex-related products. I was shopping for lingerie once and two ladies watched me purchase a hot little outfit for my girlfriend and said, "It looks like someone has special intentions." All this did was confirm that others think the way I do. So, don't think for a minute I feel comfortable purchasing a bottle of massage oil from Spencers Gifts in the middle of the mall. For those who feel the same way, try The Xandria Collection, Dept. MR0398, P.O. Box 31039, San Francisco, CA 94131-9988, 1-800-392-1777. They offer a way to order sensual products discreetly through the mail.

All this talk of women and sex brought up safe sex. *Duly noted: Unprotected sex is dangerous and could kill you.*

After hours of deliberation, our minds are full. We understand that we could discuss these issues for several more days and not cover everything. But, we compare this meeting to visiting a buffet: eating everything would be impossible. So, leaning back and smiling, as though to loosen our belts, we are content for the meal we just ate.

Meeting adjourned.

Additional Copies

PHONE:	800-247-6553
	419-281-1802
WEB:	http://single-father.com
E-MAIL:	order@bookmaster.com
FAX:	419-281-6883
MAIL:	BookMasters, Inc.
	P.O. Box 388
	Ashland, OH 44805
	USA

For e-mail, fax or mail, fill in and submit the following.

ITEM	QUANTITY	COST	TOTAL
The Ultimate Guide for the Single Father	_____	US$12.95	_____
ISBN 0–9674736–4–0	_____	CDN$19.95	_____
Merchandise sub-total			_____
Shipping & Handling*			_____
* S&H 1 copy: within US, $3.95 US$; to Canada, $6.95 US$; overseas , $8.95 US$			
Virginia and Ohio residents, add state sales tax.			_____
TOTAL			_____

Sold To

Name _____

Address _____

City _____

State / Prov _____

Zip / Country _____

Phone _____

Email _____

Cheques may be in US or Canadian dollars, payable to BookMasters Inc.

❑ Visa ❑ MasterCard ❑ American Express ❑ Discover

Credit Card # _____

Expiration Date _____

Name on Card _____

Authorized Signature _____